The Ole Days in Berkeley County, South Carolina

According to

William Dennis Shuler

With a little help from

Shirley Noe Swiesz

Author of 'Coal Dust', 'Mountain Stranger' and 'Ole Buttermilk and Green Onions'

ISBN: 0-7596-9975-5 Ebook
ISBN: 0-7596-9976-3 Softcover

This book is printed on acid free paper.

1stBooks - rev. 05/13/02

Dedication

This book is dedicated to the older people of Berkeley County, South Carolina. We are survivors! We were born before television, penicillin, polio shots, frozen food, xerox, plastic, contact lenses, and the pill. We were born before radar, credit cards, split atoms, laser beams, ball point pens, panty hose, dishwashers, clothes dryers, and long before man even *thought* about walking on the moon.

We got married first and then lived together. In our time, 'closets' were for clothes, not for 'coming out'. 'Bunnies' were small rabbits and 'rabbits' were *not* Volkswagens. A 'relationship' meant getting along with our cousins and 'outer space' was the open area behind the drive-in theater.

For us, 'time sharing' meant togetherness, not condominiums, a 'chip' meant a piece of wood, 'hardware' meant hardware and 'soft-ware' wasn't even a word. The term 'made in Japan' meant junk and 'making out' referred to how you did on your exam.

In our day, cigarette smoking was in style, (but only for *men*) 'grass' was mowed, 'coke' was a cold drink, and 'pot' was something you cooked your food in. 'Rock' music was a grandma's lullaby and 'aids' were helpers in the principal's office or something for an upset stomach. For a nickel, you could mail a letter and two post cards.

We made do with what we had and we were the last generation dumb enough to think you needed a husband to have a baby. No wonder we are so confused and there is a generation gap today!

In this book, I plan to tell you some of the things which happened in the old days in Berkeley County, South Carolina. I have tried to tell you about the south as *I* knew it. This is not a fancy tale with fancy words, but I hope I have captured the spirit of our small county in a way both country folks and city folks alike will enjoy it. I will not call *real* names as it may embarrass some good people. If you know who I am writing about, please smile and keep it to yourself, for that is what I plan to do: smile at past remembrances…and keep it to myself.

Somehow, through the depression, moonshine whiskey, revenuers, World War II and generations of crooked politicians, we have survived, and *that* is reason enough to celebrate.

A Tribute to my Family

I would like to thank my wife Jeanette for her love and consideration during our forty years of marriage. We were blessed with a daughter Sharon and twin boys, Dwayne married to Donna, and Wayne married to Wanda. We have five grandchildren, Katlyn, Natalie, Molly, Robbie, and Tyler. If I had known the grandchildren would be so much fun we would surely have had them first! A special thanks to my sisters Blanche and Adeline who encouraged me to write this book, along with all of my nieces and nephews.

Dennis Shuler

Foreword

On the front cover of this book you will find a picture of myself, Dennis Shuler, and my ole mule, 'Alice', a good and faithful animal. I believe the only way Southern folks made it out of the depression was with the help of the good ole mule. The lowly jackass labored hard and faithfully for his master, with nary a complaint. It seemed only fitting to give my mule equal space on the cover, for mules represented a life line to the farmers in the south, long before John Deere tractors came into the picture.

While traveling around different areas of the country, telling tales about wonderful, wild Berkeley County, South Carolina, a number of people have asked me to put some of these stories in writing. Not only did the old timers want to refresh their own memories, but they thought it would be a nice gesture to give future generations some insight into the lifestyle of a small-town; Southern living, the way we saw it, the way we lived it.

I spent the first eighteen years of my life in Shulerville, South Carolina, which makes up a portion of Berkeley County. Shulerville was called Palmerville until sometime in the twenties. When the US government decided to start a new post office it was called Shulerville in honor of my family. My aunt, Elizabeth Shuler Bevel Patz, was the postmistress there from 1927 to 1960. When my dad was a young man he would go to Jamestown (home of the Hell Hole Festival) and pick up the mail at the train station. He would then bring it back to Palmerville. When my aunt gave up the job, her niece Esther Lewis Brown took it over in1960 until1988. The post office was inside of my aunt's house. The government rented it in 1988 until 1989. There was no post mistress (or master) then. Post office boxes were installed and an officer in charge took care of them. In

1989 the post office was moved to Jamestown, South Carolina.

On the back cover of this book, you will find a picture of my good friend, Gamewell Brown. Mr. Brown made the moonshine whiskey trade famous in Berkeley County. This picture of Gamewell was taken beside an old, well-used, moonshine still, which can be seen on display at the Hell Hole Swamp Festival each year in Jamestown, SC.

Gamewell had his cars 'souped' up by experts and could do 135 miles per hour, easily. But ole Gamewell could out-run the revenue agents on *foot*, as well as in a car. He often had the chance to prove it, sometimes barely escaping into some swamp, to hide out until all was clear. He is now eighty years old and can be seen at the Huddle House in Moncks Corner, SC, almost daily, spinning yarns of the days of bootleggers and revenuers. He still chases women and says he loves them all, young and old. Suspicions are that Gamewell was quite a ladies' man. (Since we started this book, Gamewell has passed on to his 'reward'. I suspect he is somewhere telling his stories, though, of the good ole days... about making 'shine, outrunning revenuers, and chasing beautiful women.)

Gamewell Brown is only one of the unusual characters you will find in this book of every-day people in a bygone era. So sit back, get yourself a good strong cup of coffee and join in the fun.

By **Dennis Shuler**, *author*

Chapter One

Berkeley County is the largest county in the state of South Carolina, which consists of forty-six counties. Back in the 'good ole days', when I was a child, our county was listed among the poorest in the state. In the late thirties, when Santee Cooper, the state-owned power generating station, was born, things started changing in Berkeley County. The state-run power station began to clear the lake sites, build dikes, and prepare to generate electricity.

When the power company came to our state, many changes came about in Berkeley County. It was the ending of an era...literally the ending...many of the old plantation homes were submerged beneath the water when the dam was built, forever burying a part of our history and a way of life which was no longer useful or even working, for that matter. As old things came to an end, new things began happening. Suddenly there were jobs in our county other than working a farm or making moonshine whiskey (although some still preferred making 'shine to working a legal job)!

My father, William Elvin Shuler, was a foreman on the WPA (Works Projects Administration). The WPA was used by the government as a way to give work to the vast number of unemployed. My father and his crew were working on the dam for Santee Cooper. On the 19th of December, 1940, a falling tree struck another tree, knocking loose a limb which fell and struck my father, killing him instantly. He was 45 years old. I often think if they had hard hats back then it might have prevented his death at such an early age. All seven of us children were home with the exception of my oldest brother who was in the CCC (Civilian Conservation Corps) camp in Georgetown.

We had a little farm and we grew our vegetables and Mom spent all summer canning and drying them for winter.

We raised hogs for butchering and chickens for Sunday dinner and to provide eggs. We had a cow for milk and butter. My mother got a check for fifty dollars a month, which was a lot of money back then. We actually lived pretty well since we had learned early that everyone pitches in and does their share. My father and mother had instilled in us at an early age that we all had to work to survive and work we did without too many complaints. I guess hard work won't kill a body for my mother lived to be 96 years old.

The dam was finally built and the power company gradually became a part of our community. Small dots of light peppered the landscape as electricity snaked its' way throughout the area. One by one the small households put away their kerosene lamps, keeping them only to be used for an emergency. Electric lights became commonplace in the early forties. It wasn't long before the advent of indoor toilets...and the sad demise of the outhouse. I could write a book on stories of the ole outhouse!

During this era of time, mules and wagons were the order of the day for transportation. There were few cars on the road, for they were not affordable to most folks. The roads were all dirt except for Highway 52, which if you followed it for a few miles, would take you into Charleston. It might have been a hundred miles away, though, for in those days people living in the infamous Berkeley County area were virtually isolated from the charming, more sophisticated, city of history, Charleston, South Carolina.

When the heavy rains came sweeping down on us, the roads would become muddy and slippery, nearly impassible for a car, which would be certain to bog down or slide into the wide open ditches. A wagon, however, with its' large wheels could keep on going as the ole mule pulled it through belly-deep water.

I remember when Highway 17 A was paved, sometime around 1948. Most of the older folks thought it was a waste of good money. I don't think it was though, for look how long it has lasted! To my knowledge they haven't done a thing to it since, except fill in and black-top a few potholes, usually right before election time!

In the old days in Berkeley County, you did one of two things: you worked on a farm or you made corn whiskey. Jobs were scarce but if you could get a ride into town, and had a little money or some credit, you could buy your supplies for either purpose. I guess it was lucky for the good folks in Berkeley County that the sheriff only had one deputy, or most of us would have landed in jail at one time or the other!

We depended on the old country store tremendously. The proprietor tried to keep everything in stock a man, woman, or child, could possibly need. Inside the jumbled array of goods, you could find almost anything, from a mule collar to a pair of black patent leather shoes. (Did you know the girls in the family, lucky enough to own a pair of patent leather shoes, would use one of her mam's good hot biscuits to shine them up for 'Sunday-go-to-meeting'?) A good store-keeper also kept a vast array of liniments and ointments for the ailments which struck us all at one time or the other. And of course there were colorful cotton dress goods and thread for the women folk. If you couldn't afford store bought material, though, you could buy food for your live-stock in practically any color or design of cloth sacks which could be used to make dresses, quilts, curtains, or practically any other necessity. 'Feed sacks' they were called then and a city girl wouldn't have been caught dead in one, back then. I hear they are called 'collectibles' now, bringing in big money. Of course most country folk raised food for the live-stock on their farms, but it was pretty difficult to turn down the vivid bags of food, knowing it would serve such good purposes: appeasing the wives and giving the pigs a treat at the same time. That didn't happen too often!

3

A Sears and Roebuck Catalog was a necessity in a country home. A body could order almost anything imaginable by mail; clothes, household items, and even the supplies to build a house. There are still some old Sears and Roebuck houses around, standing strong, with an honest purity we seldom find anymore. Sears gave credit even back then and you could send a small payment by mail each month in the form of a money order. When the catalog was out-dated and replaced by a new one, we 'recycled' it and used it in the out-house. I often wonder how people managed before Sears starting sending out catalogs.

I was told that our government, during the depression years, promised every man in the country, forty acres of land and a mule. There should be a tribute to the ole mule. In my opinion, the mule saved this country from starvation during the depression, but got little recognition for it. It's a real shame so many people have gotten their pictures on stamps, but according to government records, there is not a jackass among them.

To get a mule, you must breed a mare horse to a donkey Jack. The mule is a hybrid animal and won't breed. George Washington, our first president, was also the first American to breed large Jack's to cross with his mares for mules of high quality.

In 1787, the king of Spain presented Washington with a gray Jack and two Jenny's. He also received a large black Jack and several Jennies from General Lafayette. The two strains were carefully crossbred to produce a superior Jack for mule breeding. In 1819 a gentleman from Kentucky brought a mammoth 16 hand high Catalonia Jack from overseas through the Port of Charleston. The Jack proved himself to be a good breeder and was the father of many mules before he crossed the Great Divide to Mule Heaven.

Back when I was a boy, every able-bodied family member had to work on the farm to raise food to be put on the table. No one worked alone, however, for the ole mule was his constant companion. I have a great deal of respect for that stubborn animal.

Corn was the main crop planted when I was a boy. We needed corn to grind for grits and meal for the table and to feed the hogs, cows, and chickens. We butchered hogs in the winter and salted the meat down so it would keep. When we butchered a cow, we usually got several families involved so the meat could be cooked and eaten before it spoiled. Times were hard back then but a cow or hog was never butchered that wasn't shared with neighbors and kinfolk.

Chapter Two

This gentleman called Buck was in the pulp-wood and logging business. He bought a nice tract of land in Berkeley County and moved in with his work crew. A man called Whiskey Bill was living nearby and making moonshine whiskey on the land Buck had bought. Ole Whiskey Bill knew he couldn't afford to allow anyone to move in on his whiskey-making business. Angry at the intrusion and determined to remove all obstacles, he sent one of his boys with a message to the logging man, "My pa said ta tell you when you knock off on Friday addernoon, ta take yer equipment and work crew out of the area and don't come back."

Buck went home for the weekend and began pondering over his problem. He knew Whiskey Bill had killed several men and wouldn't think twice about killing another. The law was practically useless in Berkeley County when it came to putting a stop to moon-shining. There were too many moon-shiners and too few lawmen. But the truth was Buck had a lot of money tied up in this property. He didn't want to lose his money but he sure didn't want to forfeit his life for it!

Monday morning found Buck and his men back on the job. It wasn't long before ole Whiskey Bill himself rode his horse up to the site where the men were working. Now ole Whiskey Bill was a big man who carried a big gun and was never seen without a big chaw of tobacco in his mouth. He spit long and slow, before calling the logging man by name. "Buck," he said, "apparently ya didn't git my message?" He spit again and this time the stream of tobacco landed right close to Buck's feet.

Now Buck was a small man, kind of reminded a body of one of them poets you read about in the English books. He talked quiet, almost gentle. "Mister, I got your message

6

and I know you've killed men before and have come here to kill me this morning! I'll tell you how I look at it though: I may be in hell for breakfast but mister, you can be sure that I have made arrangements for us to eat supper together tonight! I hired a man to kill you as soon as he learns I've been shot." Buck calmly turned his back to Whiskey Bill and continued working.

Whiskey Bill mulled over this for a few minutes and without a word, he left. Buck finished cutting his tract of land without any more trouble.

And so it was with the South in the old days. Sometimes men preferred to settle matters themselves and not worry about the law getting in the middle of it all.

This gentleman called Cap, was the caretaker on one of the large, sprawling plantations in Berkeley County. One of my friends by the name of Spud, lived nearby. Now Spud liked to poach on the plantation property whenever he caught the urge for fresh game. He thought he was real smooth until one day Cap caught him with a rabbit in each hand. Ole Cap called him by name, "Spud, I'm just waiting until I catch you climbing that fence with a leg on either side. That's where the buzzards will pick your bones, straddling a fence with your head blowed off." My friend never did mention going back there anymore.

I guess I will never forget the mundane things which were nothing but pure excitement to me, when I was a youngster. One such happening came about on a cold southern winter night (and it *does* get cold, even in the low-country of South Carolina). Rip Porter was in charge of a chain gang back in the old days. They sometimes camped out near our house if they were working in the area. Needless to say Rip was as tough as any man in the pack. He had to be, to control the lawbreakers he watched over. On this particular night they built a campfire to boil their coffee, cook their meal, and to keep the nippy night air at bay. One of the men by the name of Findley, had been disobedient during the day, causing trouble and confusion. After supper was over, and in accordance to their rules, the tough leader called on the other men to pull Findley down over a log with his rear end up in the air. The tough men in the chain gang held ole Findley down while Rip proceeded to give him several lashes with a bull-whip. According to some eye-witnesses, when Rip was finished with the beating, he told ole Findley to run as hard and fast as he could go. Rip gave him a few minutes head start and then turned a 'fierce, hungry blood-hound dog' loose on him. That 'wicked blood-hound' immediately picked up Findley's trail. Ole Findley hadn't run far before he climbed a tree in fear of the 'blood-thirsty' dog. The bloodhound followed his trail to the tree and gave a few long, lonesome barks. We could hear the barking clear to our house, ringing through the quiet, still night. Ole Rip finally caught the dog and let the man come down. I imagine Findley was too tired to give Rip any more trouble that night and after all the excitement, the prisoners were allowed to turn in.

Course if such a thing happened now, Findley would have a lawyer before the sun set the next day, complaining his rights had been violated! He had been 'violated' all right, but I am not sure it was his 'rights' that took the beating! And if you know anything about dogs you know blood-hounds are as harmless as they are lazy, but they have a mighty fierce-some bark!

It is possible, to my way of thinking, that perhaps we have swung the pendulum too far to the other side, when it comes to taking care of criminals. A man I know who was sent to prison said it was like a family re-union. A lot of his friends whom he had lost track, were in the prison where he was. Of course for someone who loves the outdoors and his freedom, a prison would be sure death.

A magistrate friend of mine spent a day in the prison facilities near Columbia with some law enforcement officers from Berkeley County. He later told me, "If I was a criminal and my time was up, I would commit a crime on the way home so they could send me back up there to Columbia." He said the prisoners were given three good meals a day. They had color television and clean sheets on their beds. He said he felt sure a lot of these men were living better in prison than they ever did at home.

These two reprobates by the name of Sam and Mike ran into each other at the Moncks Corner stock-yards way back when. Mike, who had the most notches on his guns took a bad cursing off of Sam. After it was over, someone asked Mike why he took all this verbal abuse in front of the crowd, when he had a gun right in his pocket. He replied, "My ma didn't raise no fool! Sam had his hand on a pistol in his coat pocket, pointed dead at me, all the while he was cussing me out! There was no way I could have out-drawn him. There will be another day, though." I guess that was what my pa meant by using 'good old horse sense'.

Now I don't know how true this story is but I feel sort of compelled to tell it just the same, since I heard it from a good source. There were these two good, Catholic, North Charleston men who had a 'thing' with each other. Regardless of their sexual preferences, they were rather dedicated to their religion. So as a special deference to their church, they made a vow they would not ply their trade on Fridays. Back then, Fridays were considered 'meatless' days. The very first Friday, the more manly of the two saw his sweetheart coming up the sidewalk with a sailor on each arm. As they approached, Ole Manly called his sweet thing aside and said, "Hey, I thought we had decided not to mess around on Fridays! We promised to keep it meatless!" Manly was pretty upset by the entire episode. His sweet little buddy replied with a smile, "This is not *meat*, my friend, this is *fresh seafood*!" Like I said I don't know how true this story is but the source was definitely a good Protestant who *swore* he didn't tell lies.

I heard tell of a woman who lived in Moncks Corner who was awful strict with her pretty daughter. Now the way I heard it the daughter liked to frequent Honky Tonks and the likes and stay out late, carousing around with wild men. But the mother was full of good motherly advice for her daughter. "Now, daughter," she would say, "if you are not in some-body's bed by midnight, you come on home! There's trouble out there after twelve o'clock!"

An old preacher by the name of Homer, told me about the time he received a frantic call on a Saturday night, from a lady belonging to his church. 'Come quickly!" She begged, "My husband is sick and may be dying!" Preacher Homer said he put the 'pedal to the metal' and when he arrived the man was lying on the floor, not moving. Homer fell to his knees and started praying. As he crouched over him in prayer, he smelled the strong scent of alcohol...white lightening! In fact his parishioner reeked of the illegal brew! Angry and disgusted, Homer stood up and informed the lady "There's nothing I can do for your husband, Madame! He is drunk as a skunk! While we are at it though, I can assure you that you can do something about these cock roaches running around your walls! Get you a can of roach spray and take care of them immediately! I think you and your man need some sanctification to clean up your lives and some sanitation to clean up your house!" Maybe you remember hearing his sermon on 'Sanitation and Sanctification'. I think he sometimes referred to it as 'cockroaches on the soul.'

A gentleman I shall call Harry was noted for making and selling moonshine whiskey. Not having a deep conscience when it came to doing anything illegal, Harry was adept at picking up any cows that might be running loose, on the side. Actually, Harry would do about anything crooked to make a dollar without working. One day, just about supper time, he and a friend were traveling on an old country road, when they saw somebody's cow walking along the ditch, heading home. Harry said to his friend, "Now, ain't that a dirty shame! Here we are riding along in this nice truck and that poor ole cow has to walk. Let's give her a ride!" They got out and loaded the cow into the truck. On the next market day, they sold her.

Ole Harry got a little braver and hired this same friend to help him catch cows at night. His friend would catch and lead the docile cows to a designated spot where Harry would be waiting. They would load them in Harry's truck and sell them the next day. It got so bad the good people of Berkeley County began tying their milk cows near their houses at night. They would tie a rope on the cow's halter and run the other end of the rope through the bedroom window and tie it to their bed. Harry's friend would brazenly cut the rope outside the window and lead the cow, rope and all, out of the yard and off he would go.

Well, Old Harry pulled into a man's yard one Sunday night to steal a few cows by himself. His friend had gone to church, being so inclined to pray for his sins at least a couple of times a year. Harry thought everybody else would be in church, too, but this homeowner by the name of Charlie was home alone. When Charlie saw what was taking place, he grabbed his high powered rifle and ran out the door, ready to fill Harry full of lead. Ole Harry was on his toes though and when he saw Charlie, he ran to his truck, revved it up and took off. Charlie jumped into his own truck, racing right behind ole Harry! After a high speed chase down the highway, Charlie got off one shot. It went through the cab of Harry's pick-up truck, splintering glass everywhere. Harry was lucky he didn't get killed.

I was telling this story one day down at the old country store and one of the men in the crowd informed me he was Harry and 'that bullet sung a song with my name on it as it whizzed right past my ear!' Scared him right into religion or so he said. The sheriff finally caught up with Harry and he spent a year or two in the state pen. I heard tell though, he never did mess around with thieving cows after the night of the 'singing bullet'. He turned to the more 'legitimate' business of making 'shine.

Chapter Three

Ole Cash, so nicknamed because he always carried a big roll of cash money on him, was heavy into the moonshine business. One day, he was invited by friends to go deer hunting down in the Hell Hole Swamp area and he accepted. His friends put him on a deer stand out by himself. After a while, Cash was surprised by a man with a stocking pulled tightly over his head. This stockinged man got the drop on ole Cash and relieved him of all his money. Although he never did find out who robbed him, ole Cash was a little more careful who his friends were after that and especially who he went deer hunting with!

A man we called Tom, said when he died not to bury him but to get a hollow log, pack his body into it and nail up both ends, then get a drill and drill holes in the log. That way he could tease the buzzards and they couldn't get to him. I wonder how long it took old Tom to come up with such an idea! Never did hear what happened to him. I suspect he was buried six feet under though and the buzzards never gave him a second thought.

Bubba Smith amazed all of us who knew him in the old days. When he was sober he was a good hearted fellow, but he loved to fight and cause trouble when he was drinking. If there was a party or a local event, you could look for him to be there, stirring things up, with a bottle of moonshine in his hip pocket. One man who grew up with him made the remark that he hoped the Lord would spare his life to see how Bubba left this old world. Let me tell you a few things I know about Bubba.

The first serious thing that happened to Bubba was in a poker game on a Sunday morning near a church in Moncks Corner. After a brief, although intense, argument with a young man, Bubba ended up being badly cut. Someone took him to the old Berkeley County hospital where the doctor sewed him up.

The next serious thing to happen to Bubba was when he got shot. This fellow by the name of Big Bart ran a small beer joint in one of the many little towns in Berkeley County. Big Bart kept his 38 pistol hanging on a nail behind the counter. One day Bubba came in the joint and the trouble began. Big Bart asked Bubba to leave. Instead, Bubba started advancing on him, the devil dancing in his eyes and a bottle in his hip pocket. Big Bart reached back and got his 38. In the blink of an eye, he put one bullet in Bubba's chest. Bubba ran out of the store and begged a bystander, "Pull my shoes off for me! I don't want to die with 'em on!" Again some good Samaritan took him to the Berkeley County hospital where the same busy doctor took care of him and he survived yet another scrape.

Big Bart was drafted into the army a short while after that and served in the European theater with the Airborne Troops during World War II. A few years after the war ended, Big Bart was deer hunting with some friends. They had just come out of the woods to eat lunch at a country store in St. Stephens when Bubba came by. He walked up to Big Bart and mockingly told him, "You shot me one time but you couldn't *kill* me." Big Bart replied in a cool voice, 'I didn't kill you then but try me today, Bubba! There will be some deep digging and low singing in your town tonight! You won't be able to stand what I'm going to give you! I have my double barrel shotgun loaded with double-ought buck shot and my trigger finger is mighty itchy!" They parted company without any further words. I heard tell Bubba settled down some after that incident.

Old Viv Singleton loved to party and dance. One Sunday afternoon he stopped by a roadside park where the Moore family was having a reunion and picnic. The Moore's had their food spread out on the table, ready to eat, when old Viv jumped up on the spread and started dancing, fried chicken and banana pudding flying left and right! One of the Moore men, appalled by Viv's drunken antics, hugged old Viv with a knife in his hand. Jess Moore opened up Viv's stomach like he was butchering a hog! Old Viv ran like a dog to the highway to try to catch a ride to the hospital. He kept stopping by the sweet gum bushes to pull leaves off and pack them into his stomach. Someone later remarked that Viv tried to stop the blood flow much like an ole bear would have done. Jess Moore finally gave in and took Viv to the hospital and saved his life after he had nearly killed him! I doubt Old Viv did much more table dancing!

Cal Whiteoak loved to speed, in the old days when he was young and full of vinegar and hot pepper. The county roads were bumpy in some places and slick as a ribbon in others, and in no condition for fast travel. Cars were not air-conditioned back then so everybody rolled their windows down to keep cool as best they could. Cal was traveling along at a fast rate of speed with his left arm stuck out of the window, when he met a log truck on one of them Berkeley County curves. Cal was a good driver but he was unable to pass the truck without a collision, thereby sideswiping the log truck and losing his left arm. They say it was a sight to see, Ole Cal standing in the middle of the road, one arm gone, acussing and ahollering! Somebody finally got him into a car and took him to the Berkeley County hospital. I heard tell after he healed up you couldn't get Cal into a car.

Old Stuart Hendricks and his nephew Slim were on a drinking spree one Friday night when they got into an argument. Things got out of hand and the nephew pulled out his knife, cut Old Stuart bad and left him to die by the roadside. Someone came along and took him to the hospital thereby saving his life. I don't think Stuart and Slim went on any more drinking sprees together.

Another good gentleman whom I know by the name of Silas Appleby, loved to hunt for deer with his flashlight. He would walk the woods roads at night, kill all the deer he could and pick them up after daylight. He sold them for $25.00 each in those days. He got caught once after daylight, in an area being used for driving with dogs. The dogs had jumped a deer and was headed toward the standers. Silas was between the deer and the standers. He was in the bushes near a pond, so he decided to try to get to the hill so he could see better. One of the standers saw the bushes shaking and thought it was a deer. He fired into the bushes. He put several buck shot into Silas and they had to rush him to the hospital. Once again the good doctor saved another of Berkeley County's citizens.

Chapter Four

Old Alvin Whitley told me when World War II ended, he enlisted in a farm school run by our government, to train veterans how to farm. They were still using mules and horses at this time as only a few men could afford a tractor.

The government paid each member a small amount by check every month to help them make a living. Alvin said jobs were scarce and this farm program wasn't really enough to support a family. Food to feed the growing family was about as low as it could get, pantries bare and empty, so Alvin decided to get up one morning well before daylight and go deer hunting. He would try to kill a deer by shining a light in its' eyes, which would hopefully blind the animal long enough for him to shoot it. He didn't tell anyone of his plan except his wife.

He walked a good distance from his house before he picked up a set of eyes. He took careful aim and pulled the trigger. He walked over and there lay a nice seven point buck. Alvin could not carry the heavy deer on his back so he went home, hitched the mule to the wagon and hustled back for his deer. After loading the deer into the wagon, Alvin trekked toward home again, happy his family would eat good for awhile. He had only gone a short distance when he got to thinking that if the ever-present game warden came along and saw the deer, there might be trouble. Just to play it safe, Alvin stopped under some pine trees and quickly picked up enough good clean pine straw to cover the deer. He arrived home with no problems. He took the deer behind the house and skinned it. He told me years later that he didn't tell anyone about killing the deer. He didn't give any of it away either, as he would have, had he killed it during hunting season. Through the good graces of illegal hunting, Alvin had enough meat to last his family for quite a spell. Such were often the ways of 'way back then'. I suspect many a man has killed deer out of season during hard times, to feed his albeit starving family. I feel it must be a frightful thing to watch your little children go to bed hungry and even a God fearing, law-abiding man would do most anything to prevent it and hunting out of season seemed the least illicit.

After World War II ended, my brother and I bought a 1940 Lincoln, twelve cylinder, sedan. It was heavy and held the road real smooth. The two of us thought we were something with that 'hot-rod' Lincoln. One night, we got together with two of our friends and decided to go night hunting in the Cordesville area. One of them had an uncle who was care-taker for a local plantation. He said his uncle was called out of town and we could night hunt the plantation without any problems.

We got a #2 washtub, filled it with ice and a case of beer. All of us were sort of high when we proceeded to the plantation. My brother was driving, and our two buddies were shining flashlights on both sides of the car. I was watching out the rear window. We were busy drinking beer and watching for deer when I spotted a car tailing us with only the parking lights burning. I sounded the alarm and one of the men took the guns and both flashlights, ran to some bushes and hid them. By the time he got back to the car, the game warden was alongside of us. He said, "What are you fellows doing out here?" My brother called him by name and said, "The same thing you're doing, trying to get us a deer!" The game warden did not answer his accusation but said,"I saw you hide your guns and lights in the bushes. You ain't killed a deer so I aim to give you a break." He grinned at us, almost beaming with self-importance. "Now git your guns and flashlights and git on out of here! I'm going on up the road and parking fer a while. I expect you fellows ta come on past me and keep going, otherwise I'll have ta arrest you." We took his advice and I have always been grateful to him, illiterate crook that he was!

18

One day a group of us were hunting down in the Hellhole area. The dogs had jumped a deer and gone. We were standing around talking when an elderly game warden drove up. As we were chatting with him, we saw an ole hen turkey run across the road. Us younger fellows decided we would surround her and shoot her when she took to the air. The game warden told us, "Don't shoot that turkey or I'll be bound to write all of you up!" We ignored his warning! A couple of us ran around the turkey and she took off flying. Just as quickly somebody put her back on the ground! Although he was very aware of what we had done the game warden did us a favor and left the area before we came back to the road.

Another game warden I knew, once told me that before he got to be game warden there was nothing he liked better than killing deer at night. He would shine a flashlight in their eyes to momentarily blind them. He said it was a thrill to him to pop an ole Doe deer on the side of her head with a load of buckshot. I really believe he was still enjoying this practice when it was convenient, when he wanted some venison steaks for supper, or when he was just looking for a 'thrill'. I don't dislike many people but I never did like this particular game warden! He was a mean-hearted person in my belief. I have killed many deer in my life, but never for the 'thrill' of 'killing'.

I was fishing one morning at Wilson's Landing with a friend when we saw this same game-warden's son fishing near the canal and across the river. The bass were schooling and he was hooking one on about every cast. He didn't even take the time to play them as he wanted to catch all he could while they were feeding on top of the water.

We put our boat in and moved over to where he was but not close enough to disturb his fishing. We caught several nice bass but he was loading his boat as fast as he could cast out his line. His father drove up and watched his boy fish for a while. He called out to him, "Are you doing any good,

Son?" The boy hollered back to his dad, "I caught a couple." The game warden got back in his car and left.

When the fish had stopped biting and the young man started to leave, we got a little closer to his boat. We could see a lot of bass in there! We decided then and there that catching all the fish you could haul in your boat was one of the fringe benefits of being the game warden's son!

Three of us, Gavin Hall, Hank Smith, and myself, were out shooting ducks one evening between sundown and dark, near the sand pit at Gravel Hill. Gavin was on the bridge and I took one side of the swamp with Hank on the Bonneau side. The ducks were flying good and we were enjoying a good shoot until a game warden approached from the Bonneau side of the swamp. Hank quickly ran into the darkened swamp, leaving his new Dodge pick-up truck beside the highway. He didn't have a chance to sound an alarm, thus causing Gavin, who was still on the bridge, shooting away, to get caught.

I stepped behind some bushes and could hear the game warden say, "Son, I may have to put you *under* the jail for this! I can charge you with shooting ducks in a state sanctuary after sundown without a duck stamp!" After putting a scare on Gavin, who had managed to do a lot of shooting without killing one duck, the game warden decided to let him go. "All I want out of you, Son, is for you to tell me who was driving the red Dodge truck by the highway!"

Gavin replied in his 'Sunday go to meeting voice', "I swear I don't know who he is, Sir," he was so sincere his own grandmama would have believed him. The game warden then asked, "Was he a big man?"

"Yes," came the 'timid, I am so sorry and I will never get caught doing this again' reply from Gavin.

The game warden said, "You can go now, Son. That truck looks just like the one the magistrate of Bonneau owns. I am going to catch that b... tonight if it's the last thing I do!" It was getting darker by the minute, but the game warden kept driving up and down the roads trying to locate the absent, innocent, much maligned, magistrate.

As the game warden made another run down the road, Hank jumped into his vehicle with me and Gavin right behind him. He cranked it up and we left the area without turning on the head lights. We all got away without a ticket, *'barely, by the seat of our britches',* as my grandmother would say.

Philip Wiggins drank heavy at one time in his life and would pass out just about anywhere. This particular day, he was loaded with 'shine and passed out in a heap on his front porch, facing the highway. Our local undertaker by the name of Harry, was passing by and saw him. Harry decided to have some fun with Philip. He turned his hearse around, eased back down the road and backed up to the porch. He got out and opened the doors to the hearse. He shook Phillip until he got him up, solemnly telling him that it was 'his time' and for him to get in the hearse and go with him. Phillip was as wild eyed as a drunken hog. When he finally realized what was happening, he laid one nasty cursing on Ole Harry. They say Phillip quit drinking right about then!

One rainy day in 1948, several of us men got together and decided to let loose some hound dogs for a rabbit chase. We had plenty of 'white lightening' and were looking to have a little fun. We were enjoying a good hunt until the dogs began giving a treeing bark. We went to them and they were holing something in the ground. One man by the name of Bob who happened to live nearby said, "Boys, I'm gonna run home and get a shovel and we'll see what's in that hole!" Within a few minutes he came back and started digging. It was not long before we saw the back of a furry animal. It was a skunk. Bob yelled, "Hold everything! I'll catch him!"

Now I knew what a skunk could do, so I put some distance between him and me. But not Bob! He caught the skunk by the tail and pulled him out of the hole.

Excited...and drunk...Bob began to swing the ole skunk around by his tail, yelling over and over, "he can't throw his musk if his feet don't touch the ground!" Everything was o.k. until the skunk grabbed hold of a bush while en route in the air. He threw his musk in Bob's face. I have never seen a man in this predicament before or since. Ole Bob cried, cursed, gagged and vomited.

One of the men in our group said, "I know what we can do to help him! Let's build a fire out of pine straw, get a good smoke going and hold his head in the smoke. This'll help clear up the skunk odor and clear out his sinus track!" We built a fire and held poor Bob's head in the smoke for several minutes and then we laid him out on the ground. Nobody, except him and the Good Lord, will ever know how close Ole Bob came to suffocating in that smoke! I do believe he was near his final resting home, but Lord Bless us, he did survive.

Chapter Five

Mack Newman owned a large farm in Berkeley County with a nice pond surrounded by trees. The branches of the trees, mostly pines, were used as a roosting place for ducks during the winter. Mack had no problem with allowing some of his friends to shoot the unsuspecting ducks, as they were coming in to roost late in the evening. It wasn't long, however, before the game warden found out about it and started hiding in the area, determined to catch the illegal duck hunters.

Now the duck hunters were a bit sore over having to run all over the place in order to dodge the game warden, so they complained to Mack. "Why, we can't even enjoy a good hunt any more!" They whined. Now I don't know if the whining got to ole Mack or if he was just bothered over the audacity of the game warden chasing *his* friends on *his* land, but ole Mack was said to have told the hunters in an even voice, "Well, just be careful. Go on about your business and shoot all the ducks you want, but you'll have to watch out for that dang game warden. If he continues to bother you, I'll just set me a trap for him. I have a pen full of hogs I'm topping out for the market. I'll shoot the b…, cut him up in small pieces and feed him to my hogs. They'll eat every scrap of him and nobody will ever find a trace of that warden on this planet earth!"

Thankfully this never happened and the game warden is still living today, but it makes one wonder...

A gentleman undertaker friend of mine owned his own funeral home. Any fool knows it's normal to put a man in a casket lying flat on his back, but my friend had a customer come into the funeral home to make pre-arrangements with a strange request. His request was this: "When you put me in the casket, I want to be naked, lying on my stomach with my rear end up. This way the whole world can kiss my naked ass!" (My friend swore on his mother's casket he was telling the truth!)

You can always tell a country girl from a city girl, or so I have been told. If they were both outside and the wind started blowing, the city girl would reach up and hold her hair with both hands but the country girl would always reach down and hold her dress tail...course that was many years ago...most women wear the pants these days, city or country, and with the advent of hair spray, they don't even have to worry about their hair.

One lady I knew said she felt bad so she went to the doctor to see if he could find an ailment for her. The doctor gave her a prescription for her woes. He could have given her some of his samples, but he told her "I can't rightly give you samples all the time. You need to take the prescription down to the druggist! He has to live too, you know!" She went to the druggist and proceeded to tear the prescription into tiny pieces right in front of him. She then threw the scraps of paper into the trash and remarked loudly, "I have to *live* too, *you know*!" To be honest this sums up the way a lot of us feel today with the price of medicine going way beyond our pocket books. '*We have to live, too*' and we welcome any samples the doctor might give us!

One man told me "According to the records, it takes only seventeen muscles to smile and forty-three muscles to frown." Like a parrot, he also told me "men lose their brain tissue three times faster than women, thereby causing them to lose their memory and reasoning, thus becoming grumpy old men!" And I thought it was being married that caused the confusion! Go figure that one, men!

A man whose name I will not mention, lived in the Jamestown area of Berkeley County. He was married four times. He lost two of his wives at different times on the railroad tracks in Jamestown. They were run down by a train. His third wife died of a heart attack at the age of thirty! He married for the fourth time and he outlived her.

The last time I heard about him, he was looking for a fifth wife! Although the circumstances were unusual no one ever questioned it.

A man I know says he had to go before the judge in Berkeley County for child support for three children. He tried to explain to the judge, since one of the children didn't look like him, he didn't think it was his child. The judge informed him he *must* keep feeding and taking care of the child and it would probably look like him when it got older. The man had no choice, he had to pay for all three children. I heard for a fact the child looked more and more like the *judge* every day!

Old Bart and Bill decided to go fishing. Bill had an artificial leg. As they put their boat in the water, they drifted a short distance from the bank and got hung up on some water lilies. Bart, who had two good legs, told his friend, Bill, to wade out into the water to get the boat untangled. Old Bill complained, "Why, I might git snake bit by a water mocassin out yonder!"

"Well yeah, you just might," Bart answered him, "but with your peg leg, you would have a fifty percent better chance than I would!"

Ole Al Chapman operated an illegal whiskey distillery in a family cemetery in Berkeley County. He let the bushes and weeds grow up in one section of the cemetery in order to hide his operations. When his father died, Al thought it best to have a talk with the preacher, telling him the situation, as the old man was to be buried right near the still. At first the preacher said he would not take part in the funeral because of the still. "Hit's a sin!" He exclaimed but later he changed his mind and preached the funeral. This family cemetery is still being used today.

Nils Smith was born and raised in Berkeley County. As a young man he went out to Salt Lake City, Utah and joined the Mormon Movement. He liked the part of the religion concerning a man having several wives. Nils came back to visit relatives in Berkeley County and I talked with him several times. Once when he made his return trip to Moncks Corner by train he wore two six shooters strapped around his waist. When he got off the train and walked up the street, he was arrested by a local officer of the law. The irate officer made him remove his guns, but being a fun loving man, Nils took it all in stride. Nils was a carpenter by trade and he could tell some tall tales about his chosen line of work. According to Nils he could saw a board so fast with his handsaw, that he would fill the air around him with sawdust. He said when the boss came to talk to him he would have to blow a whistle and wait thirty minutes for the sawdust to settle. Nils never did say anything about the wife situation though. After the sawdust story, even if he had said something I am not sure I would have believed him!

Alfred Barr was a veteran of World War I. Several years after the war ended our government decided to pay a bonus to all the veterans. After waiting for a while, Al received his bonus but his neighbor was waiting with his hand out, intent on borrowing it from him. Al loaned his neighbor, Old Geehaw, we called him, a good bit of the money with the understanding Geehaw would pay it back when he got his check on the first of the month, three weeks away.

This was during the depression years and money was scarce. When the loan came due, Al didn't see Geehaw for several days. When he finally caught up with him, Geehaw claimed he didn't have the money and asked for more time. Al generously gave him three more weeks. When the loan came due again, Al went to see Geehaw. Of course Geehaw cried poor-mouth...still no money.

Well now, ole Al was pretty tired of this mess. He went home, got his double barreled shotgun, loaded it and returned to Geehaw's house. Geehaw was sitting on the front porch, his shoes off and his big stomach poking out of

26

his shirt. Al walked up to Geehaw, stuck his double barrel shotgun into Geehaw's protruding stomach and said, "You had better bring my money to my house before the sun goes down today or there will be some deep digging and low singing in Berkeley County tonight, for I aim to kill you!" (As you might have noticed by now '*deep digging and low singing*' was a favorite expression here in the South!)

Of course Geehaw was shaking in his boots by this time. He borrowed the money from someone else to repay the loan but he made sure Al had his money before the sun went down! The strange thing about the situation was the two men lived to a ripe old age and never had any more problems. And while they weren't exactly friends, they did have a good understanding of each other. I have always been told it is best to have an understanding in the beginning and there will be less problems in the end. I always thought it was pretty good advice to live by. I expect in the end ole Geehaw felt the same way and I am sure after the incident with Al, he had no problem remembering the rules!

One man told me life was hard for him when he was growing up in Berkeley County. He had to sleep at the foot of the bed, wait to get a tater, and like many of us, he got his most lasting education out behind the barn.

This gentleman I know was one smart man! He went to his bank and drew his money out just a couple of days before the banks closed due to the Stock Market Crash in 1929. He told the banker he needed his money to buy a dairy. They gave him his money. He took it home and put it in two quart 'fruit' jars and hid it. He then joined his neighbors, crying he had lost his money along with the rest of them.

During the depression, this gentleman was able to help some of his neighbors keep up their taxes so they wouldn't lose their farms and I suspect he fed many a family. Not only was he wise but he was generous.

27

School houses in Berkeley County in the 'old days' were usually one room buildings with a large wood heater. They had one teacher per school who taught all the required subjects to all the grades. These teachers didn't have cars so they would have to board with a family near the school. In most cases they only went home for the Christmas holidays and the summer months.

Near one particular school in this area of Berkeley County, lived a good looking man who happened to be a womanizer. He would visit the home in which the school teacher was boarding and it wouldn't be long before the school teacher would come up pregnant. Practically every year they would have to send a new school teacher to the school as the current one would have to leave to have her baby... and the process would begin all over again. Things have certainly changed. Now the schools pass out condoms to the students and it is perfectly acceptable for the teacher to have an illegitimate child. And personally I think most women are too smart now to put up with such an *obvious* womanizer.

Life was difficult during the depression years. There was one man my father knew well, whose wife gave birth to twin boys during this time. He did not have a milk cow to get milk for his twins so his wife had to breast feed both babies. Of course this was a way of life then, but it was especially difficult when there were twins and the woman was not exactly well fed herself. Often times there would not be enough milk for the babies. In cases like this, the neighbors would help but they had their own to care for and could not always spare extra for others. Then it would be up to the mother to mix sugar and water and put it in a baby bottle to satisfy her little ones' hunger.

It was rough back then! But if you were fortunate you owned a farm, a mule and wagon, a milk cow to provide milk for the family, a couple of brood sows to raise your own meat, and some laying hens to get eggs. The rest of your food usually came directly from the family farm. The old country store could only carry staple goods as there was no refrigeration. Most people had little money to spend at the store anyway!

But today! We are surely living in the good times. We can turn a thermostat to get cool in the summer and warm in the winter; we can go to the 'fridge' to get a cold drink and flip a switch on the electric stove to prepare a meal in a short time. We even have indoor plumbing which was not available in the old days. And of course now the computer age has given us all sorts of things to make our lives happier, or at least easier!

During the depression many people worked on the W.P.A (which is short for Works Projects Administration). The W.P.A. was created by our president to give people jobs since the stock market crash in 1929 had really played havoc in this country. People working on the W.P.A. dug ditches and cleared right-of-ways. During cold weather, the hard working men would build a large fire near their working area. They took turns warming by this fire, even though it gave off a dark smoke and would cling to a man's face.

Ole Ike Hall was not subject to doing much work if he could get by with it. He would stay as near the fire as he could get by with doing and the smoke would literally cover him. He would leave work dirty and still be dirty when he came back the next day. A new man on the crew asked him one day if he didn't wash before he went to bed. Ole Ike remarked: "It's too dang cold to wash when I get home from work. If it don't come off on my wife's bed-clothes then it don't come off until a warm day!" Luckily the cold doesn't last too long in our part of the woods.

Chapter Six

A friend of mine by the name of Samson was determined to become a business man. He decided to begin his upward surge by building a service station. He went to the bank, borrowed money and soon had a nice little station going. But sometimes Samson got a little discouraged, like the time a customer came in and asked to use the rest room facilities. Samson gave the man the key to the rest room. The man came back, returned the key and asked Samson if he had a water cooler. My friend says "Yes, look right behind you."

After the man had drunk his fill of water he asked Samson, "Well sir, how is business today?"

Samson, a bit irritated by now, answered with a straight face, "Not too damn good! All I'm doing is trading cold water for piss!"

Someone told me the story of three old men sitting on the back steps of a nursing home, all wearing hearing aids in both ears. Things were quiet when one of the men said, "Boy, it sure is windy today!" One of the other men replied, "No, I don't think it's Wednesday. I'm pretty sure it's Thursday." The third man started to get out of his chair and said, "Yes, I'm thirsty, too! Let's go get us a drink!" The man who told me this story swore it was the truth.

The same man who told the first nursing home story told me this one too. He said there were two old ladies in a nursing home who were bored and wanted to stir up some fun. They decided to go streaking. They pulled off all their clothes and ran down the hall, passing the same three old men who were in wheel chairs this time. One man looked at the others and asked, "Did you see those ladies?"

The other man replied, "Yeah, I saw them. Their clothes sure needed pressing, though. I never saw so many wrinkles." The third one shook his head in agreement. "These young people!!"

You hear a lot about domestic problems and family fights nowadays and such goings-on reminds me of a conversation I had with the sheriff of Berkeley County, many years ago. I knew him well and one day I was in his office talking with him about things happening throughout the County. Discouraged with the world situation and especially this little County, he shook his head in a negative response. "I'm getting too old for this kind of work." One of his deputies had gotten shot in a quarrel between a man and his girlfriend the night before. Sad and feeling defeated with the modern world, the sheriff told me how he handled domestic problems in the old days. "When I received a call for help involving a family quarrel, I would wait several hours before going there and by this time they would have settled their disagreements and made up or I would have to call an ambulance to take one or both of them to the hospital. On one occasion, I got a call from one woman who said she had shot a 'peeping tom' who was looking in her bed-room window. I waited a while and when I got there I found him. He was deader than a door-nail, right under her window. I heard rumors later that he was her boy-friend. I wondered about the situation but just kept quiet. She never did give me any more trouble." The sheriff also stated he had wanted to be a sheriff since he was big enough to write the word. "Things have changed now though," he said, "if someone called me in a domestic dispute today, I would be obliged to go immediately. Yeah, things sure have changed, and many a good cop has lost his life that way!" The sheriff followed his dream and was in office for a long time but he was smart enough to know when to quit. He readily handed the job over to a younger man and went on to enjoy his retirement years.

A man called Big Joe, because of his enormous size, worked with the county road crew hauling dirt in dump trucks. It was their job to fill in the low places in the roads which washed out every time a good rain hit us. The crew was hard at work on a road when a Pepsi Cola truck came by, on the way to make a delivery to a country store. The truck got stuck in the muddy road where the men were working and try as he could, the driver couldn't move it an inch. He called on the road crew to try to push his truck by hand while he put the '*pedal to the metal*' (another Southern favorite). Finally, due to their combined efforts, the Pepsi man drove his truck out of the muddy hole.

Now Big Joe, who was a lazy sort, was endowed with a big appetite for food or drink. While the other men were pushing on the truck, he stayed behind drinking hot Pepsi-colas as fast as he could get the tops off the bottles. When the truck left Big Joe had drunk so many of the colas he could only stand there and let Pepsi flow out of his mouth. I heard tell he almost drowned in Pepsi-Cola!

I remember a certain lady who said it was her own wish, when her time came to die, to drown in Pepsi Cola! I personally don't think I would care to drown in a Pepsi or even a *Grape* soda for that fact!

Back in the old days, most women, city or country, wore cloaks. They were made of wool with fur collars and the length was either just to their knees or right below. The fur collar could be turned up around one's neck on a cold day and it would be soft and warm. The furs for many of the cloaks were trapped right here in Berkeley County. A man could stretch his meager amount of money by trapping. Often it would mean the difference between his family going hungry or having half enough to eat.

My own father was a trapper. Fur (referred to as 'hide') buyers would come to our house to buy the hides and they paid a good price for them. I remember my father getting $5.00 for a good raccoon hide during the thirties. A good 'coon dog was valuable and you could make a respectable living in the winter just hunting awhile at night. Now most of the population is afraid of rabies when it comes to racoons, but I never did hear of anyone dying from them back then. I did hear tell of a few dogs that went mad from the disease, though.

If a dog caught rabies back then, it was a nasty business. It would have to be killed and its' body burned. I once knew a man who shot a mad dog point blank several times, but it kept coming toward him. It made one last lunge and finally dropped about 2 feet from the man. That man was from Kentucky and he was one good hunter. He once killed a copperhead, he told me, way back when he lived in the mountains of Kentucky, and the bullet bounced over and killed another one. He said copperheads were all over the mountains back there. He told me that he once heard that if a mean person died, snakes would take over their home-place. He believed it was the truth for he swore he had seen it happen.

A couple of our dogs got snake bit, too, but I think it might have been by a rattlesnake or a water moccasin. We have more of them in SC than we do copper-heads and they get mighty big! When I was a kid, if our dogs got bit, Dad would pour some kerosene on the snake bite and before long the ole dogs would be back in business. It was nothing unusual for a hunting dog to get bit for a good hunting dog would sometimes go off hunting on his own and we could hear him howling way off in the distance for days at a time. Unless he got snake bit or hurt, he usually would not come home until he was physically exhausted and hungry.

Chapter Seven

There has been a lot of talk of crooked votes this last election but I am here to tell you Florida doesn't have anything on Berkeley County. A good friend of mine by the name of Will, worked the polls at one time. He told me it was a fact that as closing time drew near, friends of the politicians tried to vote every registered voter they could for the man they wanted to win. This was in the old days when paper ballots was all we had.

One man by the name of Hubert won an election at a local precinct. He went home happy as a lark, but it didn't last long. He got a phone call from a veteran politician in the city, telling him to come on out for the vote count there. Hubert said, "I have seen men win at the precinct and lose at the county seat vote count. The politicians' henchmen have been known to switch the numbers thereby letting the low man win. I know it's true for it happened to me!"

One Berkeley County man told me, "I was running late getting to the polls to vote but after arriving there, I noticed I still had plenty of time. As I stood in line, one of the poll managers came over to me and remarked, 'You can go on home now. We already cast your vote for you.' I went on home for I didn't want to stir up trouble."

I remember as a boy I was plowing a mule for an elderly man in Shulerville. One evening as we finished our work, two men in a late model car drove up and began a conversation with the old gentleman. I saw the driver of the car stick a piece of money in the old man's shirt pocket. The old man took the money out of his pocket and threw it back into the car. I don't know his exact words but he let them know his vote was not for sale.

In the old days people were told they would lose their jobs if they didn't vote a certain way. One day I stopped by an old gentleman's house and he had several cases of bonded whiskey in his living room. I knew he was an old time boot-legger so I questioned him. He said 'this here is politicians whiskey, hand delivered to me for the election! I am supposed to pass it out to the voters, but man! This is some good whiskey! A shame to give it all away!" We shared a drink or two. It *was* good whiskey! I suspect he kept the rest of it for himself.

A lady friend of mine by the name of Shirley, hails from Harlan County, Kentucky. Now Harlan had a reputation equal to Berkeley County's when it came to illegal whiskey and crooked politicians. The power company, Santee Cooper, has been buying coal from this area for many years so although many people are not aware of it, we have a close tie to the coal mining district. Shirley says she can remember when she was a teen-ager and her dad worked at a coal tipple, she would sometimes type orders for him to send out. Many of those orders went to Santee Cooper right here in Berkeley County.

Shirley was just a youngun' when two of the governor's henchmen came with money to hire her father to 'acquire' votes for the governor, via some good moonshine whiskey and baloney sandwiches. The men were dressed in fancy suits and drove an equally fancy car. They came into the little house in the coal camp, with crooked smiles pasted on their faces. Shirley watched as one of them took out a snowy white handkerchief and wiped the coal dust from her mother's chair before he sat down. The governor owned several of the dangerous coal mines in the area which hired the underpaid men to go deep into the holes to earn a meager living. Shirley's mom, like most of the other mountain women, was a very clean woman, but coal dust settled on everything in the coal camp and cleaning did little for it.

It was with an anger she never forgot which prompted Shirley to watch the men in disgust as they pulled money from their fat wallets to give to her father. She was angry at her father until he told her, "Why, Shirley, no man buys my vote. I'll buy some liquor and baloney for the voters and urge them to vote for the other man! I'll use the rest of the money to buy your school books and things your ma needs. We might have to dig coal for a living and live in mining shacks, but we don't have to sell our free will to nobody."

Chapter Eight

Bill Landers was a good friend of mine and he was an active member of the American Legion. I was shown a copy of his unusual will after he passed away. He had requested that a number of cases of good whiskey be bought out of his estate and taken to the American Legion hut to be consumed by his friends and fellow legionaries. They sent him off royally!

Aaron Wheeler was told by his 'parents' that he had been adopted when he was very young. Unfortunately they knew little about his real family or his early life. When he reached middle age, he finally located his mother who lived upstate. She filled him in on his birth and early days. She also gave him his father's name. With this information Aaron began to check around and finally located his father, a timber buyer, over in Orangeburg County. Aaron decided to ride over and have a talk with his dad. He drove up to his father's house, tooted the horn and waited for his dad to come out. Aaron had decided to pose as a man with timber to sell. After talking timber for a few minutes he told his dad who he really was. The real reason he was there was to see his father and find out what he was like. His father was shocked. Father and son had a good hour of getting acquainted and talking things over. When the time came for Aaron to leave, his father expressed sorrow that he didn't have any material goods to give to his long lost son. Aaron told him, "I didn't come to seek an inheritance. I only wanted to find my real mother and father and have a chance to talk with them for a while." To my knowledge this was their only time together. It struck me when Aaron told me the story, that his adopted parents had certainly done a good job with him!

A man by the name of Milsap was very tight with his money as he had come through the depression and knew hard times. He owned a nice farm and sold produce and livestock. After WWII he wanted to buy a new Dodge truck. He had never trusted banks so throughout the years he took his money and put it in jars and buried it in the chicken house under the roost. The chickens' waste kept the jars covered. His theory was no man in his right mind would look under the roost in a chicken house to hunt money. As things turned out he was right. He bought his truck and I rode to the market with him several times.

One Saturday afternoon his son, Guy, drove up to his father's house, to find him sitting in a chair in the back yard with a gun across his lap. A surprised Guy asked what the problem was. Milsap replied, "Look at all those one hundred dollar bills hanging on the clothes line and you'll see my problem!" He had opened the jars and found some sort of fungus on them. He washed the stained bills to get them clean, and then hung them on the clothes line with clothes pins, to dry. He told his son he was sitting with a shotgun just in case anybody came along and tried to rob him. I have been told by older people that burying money is a bad policy. If you fall into this category, I suggest you check it out, especially if it is near a chicken house!

Maynard Hill got a job at the Port of Embarkation during World War I. He hired in as a carpenter. He made out well for a few days until the boss asked him to climb up a ladder and measure a board on top of the warehouse. His boss called up to him, "How long is the board?" Maynard, who could not read a measuring tape replied, "Two hammer handles, one hand saw, and three nails." The boss said, "Come on down mister, I can't use you any longer."

Billy-Bob Helton wanted a job at the navy yard during World War II. He contacted his uncle in the Charleston area, to help him get a job there. His uncle told Billy-Bob to come on to town and he could stay with them. The young man packed his cardboard suit case and started hitchhiking to Charleston. When he got there, his aunt gave him a room but told him he would have to take out a five thousand dollar insurance policy and make them the beneficiaries, since they were caring for him. Billy-Bob agreed to this. Almost immediately his two cousins started plotting on how they could collect the insurance.

The cousins kept after Billy-Bob to go swimming with them. He finally decided to go and as they were playing around in the water, one of them cut Billy-Bob's heel string in hopes he would drown. After waiting a while and he didn't bleed to death or drown they took him to the doctor. He was still not suspicious of the cousins. After all they were *kin*.

Later on they talked him into taking a few drinks with them. Billy-Bob said he was on the back seat and his two cousins were on the front. They kept passing him the bottle. It was dark and he laid over on the seat and had nearly passed out, when he heard his cousins talking. They had driven down a dark, isolated, dirt road. He heard one cousin tell the other, "We can't kill him in the car! It will make too big a mess!" Billy-Bob was wide awake now but pretended to sleep. Worried and scared, he began to look ahead for some type of landmark. He finally saw an old store up ahead with a flood light out front. He raised up in the seat and told them, "Stop at the store. I need me a chaser so I can take another drink." When they pulled into the bare, packed dirt that served as a parking lot, Billy-Bob jumped out and ran inside the store. The owner was behind the counter and Billy-Bob, breathless with fear, told him, "Help me, those men are trying to kill me!"

The store owner, thinking Billy-Bob was just another drunk looking for trouble, replied, "My wife is sick and if you don't shut up and get out of here I am going to kill you myself!" Billy-Bob ran out the back door into a cornfield. He laid flat on the ground as his cousins pulled their car up to the fence and shined the headlights into the field, trying to locate him. Billy-Bob stayed there all night. The next day he walked through the fields and woods until he found a road. He started hitchhiking and was picked up by a pulpwood truck. He made it back home and forgot all about the navy yard. When he told me this story, I couldn't help but wonder if his kin ever had a family re-union!?!

A man by the name of Marsh owned a small farm adjoining a spiteful neighbor during the depression. Marsh was having a struggle to raise his family. His neighbor, careless of others' rights, allowed his hogs to run loose in neighboring fields. Now Marsh talked with his neighbor in nice terms about his roaming hogs, but to no avail. He decided to try another way. He told him, "You have a choice, either keep your hogs out of my fields or I am going to shoot them."

The hogs kept coming so Marsh started shooting them. After church services on a Sunday morning Marsh was standing in the churchyard when he happened to look in the direction of his home. A large black smoke was rising into the atmosphere. He shouted to his friends, "My house is on fire!" When he got home he found his barn and stables burned to the ground, with the horses still inside. It was suspected the neighbor did it, but it could not be proved. Things often got bad during the depression and this was a terrible example.

In those old days about the only real recreation for the older people was a good square dance at one of the homes. Old Mack Campbell said he was at such a dance and enjoying himself immensely, 'cutting the rug' and chewing his tobacco to the tune of the music! The windows in this home, old type shutter windows, were wide open. When Mack needed to spit out his tobacco juice, he would dance close to one of the open windows and let it rip! On this particular occasion, he had a mouthful of juice and let it fly as he waltz passed the window. To his surprise, just as he spit, a man looked into the window. Old Mack's tobacco juice covered the man's face! This started a free-for-all fight and ended the dance. I suspect the fight was enjoyed more than the dance, though.

Wooden shutters were common in our small Southern communities and so were fights. On one occasion at another shuttered house, a ruckus was started in the middle of a dance. Old Hal Creech said he had sharpened his knife before leaving his home, just in case. Well, when the ruckus started someone blew out the kerosene lamps and out came the knives. Hal said he ducked under a bed by a window when he heard a man holler out, "Who the hell cut me?" Just a few seconds later he heard him call out again, "Who cut me this time?" Several men were badly cut in the darkness and people began trying to find their way out of the house. Several people jumped on the bed Hal was hiding under and out the window they would go, shutters rattling every which way. Hal said he laid under the bed, not moving and barely breathing, until everything was over. He then jumped out the window and went home without getting cut or hurt in anyway. I suspect there was blood on his newly sharpened knife, though.

Antsy Whitaker loved to drink moonshine whiskey and ride around on the weekends. He had an old model 'A' ford and kept a jar of moonshine in his car about all the time. Some weekends he would get his brother-in-law and they would go to the sea coast to whoop and holler and pick up fast women! They were both womanizers and could tell some tall tales about their experiences. One day Antsy was headed home when two teen-age boys thumbed him for a ride. He knew them, so he picked them up. When he got to this brother-in-law's house, he told them to stay in the car. "I won't be long and then I'll take you boys home," he told them.

He left his jar of whiskey and coca-cola chaser in the car. These boys decided to have a bit of fun at Antsy's expense. They drank half of the coca-cola and urinated in the bottle, filling it up again. When Antsy came out he reached for his bottle of moonshine and took a big swig. He swallowed an equal amount of the 'Coca-cola' chaser. The boys were a bit worried now, but ole Antsy merely remarked, "Boys, if I didn't know better, I would swear that was piss!"

Old Mic Henry was known as one of the best deer hunters in Berkeley County. I had the privilege of hunting with him on quite a few occasions. He lived near us when we were growing up. He raised a large family of seven boys and five girls. It was always a pleasure to hunt with him and listen to some of the old tales and folklore from yesteryear. I remember him saying he would rather hunt as a group of four hunters instead of a crowd. He said then you could figure on a quarter of a deer when you killed one. He had hunted all his life and knew the woods and the runs the deer would take, like the back of his hand. He could always put you on a stand that would pay off.

On several occasions when Mic was up in age, he would stay in the road and tell us where to go in the woods to shoot a deer. He would describe to you how the stand would look and when you got there, he would be right on target.

He hunted quite a bit by himself. He had a little red horse he would ride, with his dogs trotting along beside him. I have seen him going by our house early in the morning and later on in the day, he would come back by with a deer tied behind the saddle.

He told me as a young hunter, he would watch for deer tracks and trails in the woods. He would hunt with dogs and when they struck trail he would find a place that looked good to him and wait. He would stand there until the dogs jumped the deer. If the deer didn't come by him then he would search the dirt roads until he found the running tracks where they had crossed. He would wait two days and then go back to his hunting place and turn the dogs loose.

Usually the unsuspecting deer would have gone back to his old habitat.

When the dogs struck trail, Ole Mic rode his horse to the place where the deer had crossed two days before. He would tie his horse out of the way and get ready to shoot. His theory was that a deer, being a smart animal, would figure out if he was molested once and had gotten away, then he would make the same run which had saved him before. Mic killed a lot of deer by himself in that manner.

Lots of times Mic would take the dogs or send a man to an area where he thought a deer might lie down. He was usually right and the scent of dogs or man would get the deer moving quickly. This would always save time in jumping a deer. Old Mic was smart when it came to living off the land. I guess what made an impression on me was Old Mic's respect toward the creatures he killed. He didn't kill for the fun of it but to feed his family or help his neighbor's feed their own.

A good Christian man by the name of Les Helton had lived in Shulerville all of his life. He made his living by farming and raising hogs and cattle. He would gladly help anybody and I had the privilege of plowing a mule for him when I was just a boy.

Since Les was the last man living on the old country road, he would let his hogs and cows graze open range. Open range for livestock was a way of life in those days and it would be necessary for a farmer to fence up his fields in order to protect them from the animals. This was the law. Les would build hog pens in different areas of the woods and put a brood sow, heavy with pigs, in each one and in this way, when she gave birth to a litter of pigs, she would not leave them. Les would take bags of ear corn, tie them behind his saddle and ride his horse to these pens every evening for a while. As the hogs got adjusted to their new home, he would feed them less frequently.

He raised a tough breed of hogs that could survive in the South Carolina swamps. They would root under bushes and eat herbs until the acorns started falling in the autumn of the year and then they would become fat from eating them. This breed of hogs was called Herefords. They resembled a white face Hereford cow and Les was the only man I knew who raised them.

As the young hogs grew and matured, Les would put ear corn in the pens and leave the door open. They would go in and eat the corn as he called to them. In this way they would stay adjusted to his scent as well as his call.

When the hogs were grown, Les would feed them in the pen as usual, but while they were eating he would shut the door. He had a large cage on his wagon, pulled by a mule. He would catch the hogs, load them in the cage and take them home. Once they were penned up at home he would feed them corn and fish meal until they were fat enough to butcher or send to the market.

Some of these young hogs would stray off in the woods and not come back. They actually went wild and were scared of humans. This created problems so Les had to train dogs to find and catch them. He kept a very mean dog aptly named Butcher, who would go on a wild hog, catch him by the nose or ear and hold him until Les could take over.

Some of the wild hogs had long tusks protruding from their mouths. If the dogs weren't careful they would be cut to death by the vicious boars. When a dog was cut badly Les would sew him up, give him time to heal, and before long the ole dog would be catching hogs again. This was a way of life and an honest living for Les.

Chapter Nine

I once knew a very large man. He had an enormous stomach that stuck way out in front. He wore a large, wide belt to hold his stomach in as much as possible. When he pulled the belt tight, his stomach would protrude over and under the belt. His sister-in-law called him 'the man with two bellies'. He was never offended by it. I guess laughing at ourselves helped us all to get through the hard times.

Back in the good ole days most country people raised Blue Ribbon sugar cane to make homemade syrup. In the fall of the year when it was time to make the syrup, they would strip the leaves off the stalks of cane, cut it down, and haul it to a cane mill in the community.

The cane mill was made of metal cylinders that rotated together as it was being pulled by a mule traveling in a circle around it. It had a wooden beam hooked to it and the other end hooked to a mule. As the mule walked around in a circle, rotating the cylinders, somebody had to feed the stalks of cane into the cylinders, thereby squeezing the juice out of the cane which ran into a tub. When the tub was full, it would be emptied into a large vat. When the vat was full, a fire was built under it to cook the juice until it became syrup. The juice could not be cooked too fast or the syrup would have a scorched taste. It had to be skimmed regularly while it was cooking to deter the foamy skim that appeared.

A young boy, not much over eleven years old, by the name of Vic Hornsby, was helping his family with grinding cane by feeding the stalks of cane between the cylinders. Everybody was busy and didn't see what happened until the young fellow started hollering and crying with pain and fright. He had held onto a stalk of cane too long and his hand and arm went between the cylinders, crushing and twisting in an agonizing bend. They rushed young Vic to

45

the hospital and amputated his arm above the elbow. He survived the tragedy and by the time World War II started, he was old enough to get a job at the navy yard. He was fitted with an artificial arm and trained to weld. Vic worked at this trade until he retired. He now lives near Columbia and operates a small nursery. I have always admired Vic for his determination to live a normal life in the face of what might have been a disaster for him.

Jeff Jones was just a teen-ager of 13 or 14 when the depression came. His father owned a large farm in upper Berkeley county and a barber shop in town. One morning as they left home and headed for the barber shop, they saw a man with a hog tied down, by the roadside. Jeff looked closely as they passed and told his father "Daddy, that's one our hogs!" His father kept going but remarked in a sad voice, "Son, it is one of our hogs but I don't want to tangle with that man. He has a mean reputation. He thinks nothing of stealing hogs and he has the same attitude about killing a man!" The stealing continued and Jeff's father still didn't do anything about it. After fighting a difficult situation for many months, Mr. Jones sold his farm and moved to North Charleston. I don't think he was a cowardly man, he just had the good sense to know when he couldn't win. Jeff told me later that his father felt his family's welfare came before everything else, even his pride.

A man I shall call Bo was very jealous of his pretty young gal friend, Liza. One night at the Macedonia high school, during one of the cake walks, Liza decided to walk with another man. In vicious anger, Bo pulled out his pistol and shot the man in the leg. The man recuperated from the pistol wound and served in the army during World War II. I don't know what happened to Bo. A lot of good men have died over the most ridiculous of reasons, and jealousy is right up there with greed. Come to think of it a lot of wars having been fought for the same petty acts, jealousy and greed.

Tom Tomkins was the owner of a store in Berkeley County that sold about everything a person needed. So when Bart Knowles sent word he needed a large amount of fertilizer and other farm supplies, Tom was aware the man had a bad reputation for not paying his bills, as well as being mean as sin. When his delivery man, Al Hambrick, loaded the requested amount of fertilizer and goods onto his truck, Tom instructed him, "Do not unload anything until you get paid in cash." Tom handed him the bill for Al to take to Ole Bart.

When Al was back several hours later with an empty truck, Tom was happy and a bit relieved. With a smile of satisfaction on his face, he went to collect his money from Al but the frightened driver told him, "I didn't collect a penny. I told Bart Knowles I would have to be paid before I could unload anything. He said he had the money in his pocket and would pay as soon as I unloaded the goods. I backed the truck up to his shed and he helped me unload it. As soon as we finished, Bart told me to get off his property or he would put a whipping on me. I'm terribly sorry, Mr. Tomkins. I didn't get a cent of your money." I was told Tom never did get his money and Al quit driving a truck and found a more peaceful way of earning a living!

This gentleman by the name of Frank Poston was well up in age but still loved to deer hunt. One day as he was hunting down in Hell Hole Swamp with some friends, a large buck ran out and he quickly shot it. As was his custom when he downed a deer, Frank walked up to the ole buck lying on its' side, and stepped one foot over the carcass. He caught it by the horns with his left hand and with a knife in his right hand, he reached down and cut the deer's throat. To Frank's surprise, the old buck wasn't dead! Determined to get away, the big buck jumped up with Frank on its' back holding onto its' horns. The ole buck was petrified with the man on his back and Frank was too scared to turn loose of its' horns. After bouncing around for a time, Frank was finally thrown off the deer. He began hollering for help. Some of his friends came to his aid. The ole buck only went a short distance before he fell dead. Frank was unhurt although he was terribly shook up. He said he had hunted all of his life but this was the first time something so bizarre had happened to him. I have seen deer on several occasions get up after being shot and manage to get clean away.

A young gentleman by the name of Herman loved to drink corn whiskey back in the old days. On a particularly cold winter day, according to his pretty wife, she had a large pot of homemade soup on the wood-stove ready for dinner, when Herman came home, higher than a kite. She had just taken the lid off of the pot when Herman came into the house, 'feeling his oats'. He pulled off his shoes and socks, and threw his socks up into the air. One of the dirty, stinking socks fell into the pot of soup. Being drunk, he didn't notice. His wife later told us, "I was so mad, I didn't bother to take the sock out of the pot of soup. I gave him a large bowl full with the sock still in it. He tried to bite into that ole sock, thinking it was some tough meat! He couldn't do much with it, so he simply ate the rest of the soup and left the sock, still thinking it was tough meat!" He survived so I guess it goes to show that a stinky sock won't kill a body if it's mixed into a good pot of soup! I might also add that it doesn't pay to mess with a woman who has worked hard over a hot stove all day while the man is out having a good time!

Art Johnson operated a large store in the ole days. He sold about anything you needed for that era of time. Well, it so happened James Tidwell was planning to build a house and he turned to Art for the supplies. He needed lumber, nails, windows, doors, and tin for the roof. Art had everything James needed for his house but it was only after he had gotten the materials together, that James told Art, "I don't have the money to pay you, but I'll get it together in a few days."

Well, Art didn't want to have any trouble with James so he said 'alright'. James built his house and still made no effort to pay the store-owner. Finally Art figured it was time for him to have a talk with Mr. Tidwell.

James' house was built down a dirt road with a gate across the entrance. The gate had a lock but it was not fastened. Art got out of his car, opened the gate, drove in and then shut the gate behind him. When he arrived at James' house, James had a fire built in the front yard and sat beside it, warming himself.

Art said he was greeted very warmly, asked to have a seat and they talked for a while. After they had enjoyed a good visit, Art asked James for the money he owed him, or at least a part of it. James said, "You go back to your store and I'll be there in a short while to pay you."

Art Johnson started to leave and James said he would ride as far as the gate and open it for him. Being a good-hearted soul, Art felt this was a good deed on James' part. When they arrived at the gate, James got out of the car and opened the gate for Art. When the store-keeper drove through the gate, James called out for him to stop. When he did, James proceeded to lay a cursing on Art. He said, "You have a nerve coming to my house and asking me for money! I should pull you out of the car and stomp you into the ground. Don't ever come back to my house asking for money as long as you live!" The store-keeper feared for his life and left as fast as he could. He never went back and he never collected his money.

Chapter Ten

Andy Harris was a pretty rough individual. In his younger days he engaged in a rough and tough 'fight to the finish' with his cousin, Buddy, who was also a very tough customer. After a hard battle, Buddy was winning the fight so Andy's brother opened a knife and handed it to him, yelling, "Cut him! Cut him!" Andy cut his cousin severely, ending the fight.

They took Buddy to the doctor and had him stitched up. I have no doubt the doctor did his best, but in a few days Buddy died, either of internal bleeding or infection or maybe both. Andy left town and didn't come back until he was an old man.

Berkeley County was a rough place back then, and senseless fighting took many lives. Often the fighting took place between relatives and caused hard, bitter feelings within the family.

A man by the name of Ace, was a big time bootlegger and loved fast cars and horses. I was told by several people that he could drive a car in reverse about as fast as it could go in those times.

He bought an ex-race horse and she was a beauty. Ace loved the horse and rode her often. One day he was riding her on an old woods road at top speed. As he rounded a sharp curve, probably throwing all his weight on one stirrup, the leather strap holding the stirrup broke, causing him to lose his balance and fall headlong into a pine tree.

He was found by the tree, unconscious. The bark was knocked off the tree where he hit it as he slid to the ground. Someone found him and took him to the hospital but the doctor could not save him. I guess it was just fast Ace's time to go.

The horse was bought later by a friend of mine, Allen Long, and used on his farm. I saw Allen work her and she

50

never gave him any trouble. He said she was a good horse both in working and riding.

Two men whom I knew well, engaged in a fight which was the talk of the county for many years. This story was told by a man who was there and saw it all happen: Billy Hostetter was a care-taker on a large plantation in Berkeley County. He would frequently ride his horse on the plantation to check on things as any good caretaker would do. There was a lot of poaching going on in those days.

A group of men were deer hunting in the area. They said their dogs ran a deer onto the plantation land, causing the caretaker to come after them. Hot words were exchanged over the situation, each accusing the other. The fellow who acted as spokesman for the group, Brian Wilhoit, was exceptional with his feet in a fight. He wore leather boots most of the time. Billy, the caretaker, was good with his fists, as he had boxed some. Seeing there was going to be trouble, someone collected all the guns and put them beside an old building. The two were told nobody would get a gun so they would have to settle the disagreement with their fists.

They began fighting and one man said he had never seen a man who could kick like Brian Wilhoit! The caretaker was shorter than Wilhoit, with a heavier build, and he was taking a lot of physical abuse around the lower part of his stomach from Wilhoit's boots. The fight had to be stopped and Billy managed to get on his horse and head home. Although he didn't go to a doctor, evidently he was in a lot of pain when he arrived home. He went to his bed and never got up again. He died a few days later from gangrene setting up in his stomach. Brian Wilhoit sold his farm and moved to another county. He lived to a ripe old age before he died of natural causes. It is sad to me that a fight over something so simple could cause the death of a good man, and the outcast of another.

A gentleman by the name of Mack was born and reared in Berkeley Country. He was a big time bootlegger and during World War II, he was elected mayor of a small town outside of Berkeley County. Mack had one highway patrolman tied into his operation.

He reportedly used army ambulances to transport his whiskey. During the war, who would suspect an army ambulance of doing anything but transporting wounded servicemen??

His operation, although smart and unusual, was like all other moonshine whiskey operations: sooner or later they got caught.

This went on for quite a while before anyone became suspicious. The bootleg operation had tight security with the mayor and the highway patrolman running the show. The local lawmen simply could not find the evidence they needed to arrest them.

Finally, the FBI was brought in with a black FBI agent from Washington DC, sent to work the case. Southerners were not accustomed to seeing a black lawman. The confident bootleggers didn't give it a thought when a black man started buying car loads of illegal whiskey. He had a camera and secretly took pictures of their operation. It was so simple it was difficult to actually believe. The black FBI man had the facts on them and both the mayor and the highway patrolman were arrested. They were summoned to appear in federal court in the fall of 1945 at the Federal Building in Charleston. I had just returned home from Italy and a friend of mine asked me to go with him to hear the case as the mayor was his first cousin.

I don't remember the exact sentences but both were convicted and sent to Tallahassee, Florida to serve time. The ex-mayor came back to the Bonneau community after his prison term was completed. He got his life together, married his childhood sweetheart, who was a widow at the time and they lived 'happily ever after'. He lived to an old age and was a faithful member of the church until his death. I have heard it said by the old people that ex-crooks sometimes make the most credible church-goers as well as upstanding members of their community.

Bob Henry was left handed and well built physically. He enjoyed a fight and was good at it. He had a couple of friends and they were all hanging out on Bonneau beach, drinking corn whiskey, sleeping in their cars, what little time they slept, and not taking care of themselves. One evening a highway patrolman drove up to the pavilion and said something Bob didn't like.

They had words and Bob told the patrolman to pull off his badge and gun and he would 'whip his butt'. They were both about the same build but the patrolman was more physically fit. The two of them walked down on the beach and began to slug it out. The patrolman won the fight but had Bob been sober, I would have bet on him.

Oscar Hamilton, a friend of mine who happened to be a magistrate's constable, loved to hang out at the Bonneau Beach pavilion. He was proud of his little thirty-two revolver and kept it in a holster hanging from his belt.

One night Craig Littleton had been drinking and he just reached over and pulled Oscar's pistol out its' holster. He put it in his pocket and asked Oscar what he was going to do about it. The constable begged and pleaded with Craig to give back his gun.

After letting him beg for a while, Craig gave the gun back to Oscar. The constable was a relieved man when he got the pistol back into its' holster. When carelessly carrying a gun in a open holster in a crowd, this could happen to anybody.

A man by the name of Ward was a very rugged individual and good with his fists. He would fight with a smile on his face. His brother, Bert, operated a little café in a small town in Berkeley County. On Saturday nights, Bert would keep his café open way past midnight. Some of the people who lived close by, had been complaining about the loud whooping and hollering that went on until the wee hours of morning. On this particular night somebody got in touch with the mayor and he went to the café and asked Bert to close up for the night.

Ward was pretty mad. He knocked the mayor down on the floor, jumped on him and started beating him up. He didn't realize the situation was out of hand, until the mayor got his pistol out of his pocket and shot him several times in the chest. Ward died on the scene. The mayor left town later and lived the rest of his life in another county.

This gentleman by the name of Howell was a rough one and had killed several people with his old thirty-eight pistol. He liked to go to square dances and he had two good looking nieces who usually went with him. A young man from the state of Virginia was down in Berkeley County working on the Santee Cooper Dam. He was attending the square dance at the same time Howell and his nieces were there.

The young Virginian was fascinated with one of the nieces and danced with her several times. Then, for no apparent reason, she wouldn't dance with him anymore. He questioned the beautiful young lady and she told him her uncle said she couldn't dance with him again. The Virginian went over to her uncle and asked why he did not want his niece to dance with him.

Without answering the young man, the older man swung on him, but the Virginia man was tougher. He knocked Howell down. Lying flat on his back on the floor, Howell pulled his thirty eight pistol out of his pants pocket to shoot the young Virginia man. Before he could get a shot off though, the young Virginian kicked the gun out of Howell's hand and it went sliding across the floor. The man from Virginia let Howell get to his feet and then he proceeded to beat his face to a pulp. Some friends finally had to lead Howell off the dance floor and take him home.

54

This was one time Howell lost a fight even though he had his pistol in his pocket.

He might have learned a lesson, but it did not stop him from being mean. He still put his trust in his old thirty-eight revolver and you could bet when you saw him that he had it in his coat pocket or under his shirt.

Chapter Eleven

Three men I knew well, by the name of Mike, Bill, and Lige decided to go fishing one night at the power house on the Tail Race Canal. They knew there was a lot of *big* catfish swimming around in front of the locks where the water was let out into the canal.

They got their fishing gear and slipped into the canal after dark, when they thought no one was watching. The game-wardens were doing their job, however, and it wasn't long before they had the three men surrounded. Their choices were to get caught and pay a fine, or jump into the swirling dark waters pouring out of the locks and swim for it.

Mike and Bill decided to stay with the game-wardens but Lige determined to take his chances. He dived overboard. He later told me the water was terribly swift coming out of the locks and it quickly pushed him down stream. It was a scary experience and one he never wanted to repeat, he told me. When he was finally able to make it, he swam to the edge of the canal, got out on the bank and walked the railroad tracks home, sopping wet.

Word was out the next morning that ole Lige had drowned. Later in the day, to our relief, we learned he had made it home in one piece, although frightfully shook-up.

Disgusted with her weight, Lady-Mae looked into a full length mirror. The front view was large and when she checked her side view, it, too, was large. So was the rear. She started on a diet and in a few days she decided to go on two diets as she was not getting enough to eat on just one. She is now on three diets.

Ole Mince Moore worked for a small dairy in Berkeley County. Mince was one tough fellow. He did all the milking by hand. He would set the bucket down under the cow and milk her with both hands. The owner had modern equipment for milking but Mince said he preferred the old fashioned way since he didn't care much for new-fangled things.

One morning I stopped by the dairy to get a young calf. It was cold and frost was on the ground. Mince was walking around the dairy barefooted.

He loved to run gill nets around Lake Moultrie in the spring of the year when the Crappie came into the shallow water to spawn. He said the game wardens nick-named him "Old Bear".

One moon lit night he had his nets out and was bringing in the fish right and left! He kept a watchful eye on the shoreline for any movement that would signal he had company. The ever vigilant game-wardens were watching for men using nets.

Mince said he noticed a slight stirring on the shoreline. He kept watching and listening very closely. Sound travels clearly over the water when all is quiet. He heard one game warden say to the other, "We've got Old Bear in a trap tonight. He can't get away this time!" Mince said he began pulling his net up slowly, gently paddling his boat away from them, while they waited for him on shore. They did not have a boat so he outfoxed them again. He said, "I changed my tactics a bit and was still able to catch and sell fish."

Mince ran a store which sold non-game fish but he was perfectly willing to sell game fish to anyone he knew well. I could always get fish from him when I wanted them. He told me a story one day about an incident he had with one of the wardens.

A man came into his store one night and asked to buy enough crappie or bass to have a fish fry for his family. He really put up a good talk and had no markings on his clothes as being a warden. Mince was a little suspicious and asked the man, "Are you a game-warden?" The man's answer was "No, Sir, I just want some fish for my family to have a good fry." Mince weighed out enough game fish to satisfy him. The man paid for his purchase and went out the door. In just a few minutes he returned, pulled his badge out and consequently wrote Mince up for selling game fish.

Mince told me he had a loaded thirty-eight pistol under the counter in front of him and he started to fill the warden's back full of lead as he started out the door. He told me in all seriousness, "I don't mind getting caught red-handed but to be deceived in such a manner is not my style." I got to know Mince well as he moved into my area after leaving the dairy but eventually when his health began to fail, he moved to North Carolina to be near his daughter. He was one tough ole man who lived by his own rules, but he made a point never to hurt anyone in the process, if it could be avoided.

A gentleman stopped at a seven/eleven store in Goose creek one afternoon after a shower of rain. A young woman was behind the counter so he thought he would make conversation with her. He said to her, "Lady, it looks as if you just had a shower." She replied, "You —— I'll have you know, I take a shower every day!"

A man I knew by the name of Bass, was a magistrate and had a good friend on the highway patrol. They decided to make some fast money, or so I was told, and they got a moonshine still going. This was in the early 1950's. They hired someone to run the still for them while they took care of buying supplies and finding a buyer for the whiskey.

I don't know how long they were in operation but I was told the Revenue Agent caught their worker at the still. He didn't try to run or get away. They were surprised at his calm demeanor when he was told he was going to jail. He said, "You can't take me to jail! I am making whiskey for the magistrate and a highway patrolman!" To my knowledge there was not any evidence against them except this man's testimony.

Bryant Wheeler loved to drink corn whiskey and have a little fun. He was a good fellow but sometimes when he got to drinking he would get into a little trouble. One night he and some friends were having a party near a small lake in Berkeley County. They saw some cows in a pasture nearby. The men were all pretty drunk when they decided to butcher one of the cows and take some fresh meat home with them.

The farmer who owned the cows lived not far from the pasture. He heard the men hollering and laughing all night, but he just figured they were having a good time drinking and carrying on. But when a cow came up missing from his pasture the next day, he began looking in the area where the disturbance had taken place. He found where the cow had been butchered. Blood was everywhere. Since the drunken men didn't have any way to hang the cow up in order to skin it, quite naturally the meat would be dirty after being cut up on the ground. The law was called in and they soon came up with names of the 'cow-nappers'.

The constable drove out to check on one of the men, which happened to be Bryant. As he pulled his car into the gravel driveway, Bryant came outside and walked over to the car smiling, as cool and casual as could be. The constable told Bryant what he had come for; he wanted to check out Bryant's freezer. Still smiling Bryant said, "The only way you can look into my freezer is to have a search warrant!" The constable replied, "I figured as much, so I brought one with me." After showing him the search warrant, the constable followed Bryant into the house.

The constable went to the freezer, raised the lid and saw a whole mess of dirty meat in it. He asked Bryant where he had gotten the meat. Bryant, trying to brazen it out, replied, "My wife *bought* that meat at the Piggly Wiggly." The constable patiently told him, "You know the Piggly Wiggly don't sell meat that looks like that, Bryant!"

A case was made and Bryant came up for trial in the next term of court. At the advice of his lawyer the case was settled out of court after Bryant agreed to pay for the cow.

I knew everyone involved and was glad to see things settled in a civil manner. Whiskey can sure cause a lot of heartache, headaches, and problems for any family. Bryant was basically a good, fun-loving person who got caught up in a bad situation.

Old Roger Porter owned a nice farm in Berkeley County and he liked to do a little hunting now and again. One Saturday afternoon he decided to go squirrel hunting with his dogs. He had cut timber on his property several months before which left several old stumps lying around. He told me his dogs were trailing around those stumps, so Roger, being the lazy sort, decided to squat down and lean back against a dogwood tree, his double barrel shotgun across his lap, and take a little nap. Just as he had dozed off to sleep, a large black cat jumped out of a stump on top of one of his dogs and before Roger could move, had killed it. Next, he jumped on Roger, leaving long, deep scratch marks on him as well as on his gun. It scared poor ole Roger so badly he went into shock.

His wife found him walking around the yard in a daze and took him to the doctor. It was several days before Roger got over the 'black cat' episode. After showing me the scratch marks on his shotgun, ole Roger took me to the spot where the cat jumped him. Some of the men laughed about it but a man who had lived there before Roger, told me he had seen those black cats when he was traveling the deserted, dead end road at night.

Several of us got together with shotguns and walked the woods over there but we never ran into any of the cats. It is possible they left the area after being disturbed by dogs and man. It is my own suspicion the cat was as scared as old Roger Porter that fine day!

There were other incidents of cat attacks about the same time. A Berkeley County farmer was walking out in his broom grass field one day when two large brown cats jumped out and behaved as though they were going to attack him. He said he was scared half to death as he didn't have his shotgun with him. He said he was one relieved man when the cats decided to move away from him.

Several days later a lady by the name of Mary, who lived near Macedonia High School, was awakened one night by her dogs barking wildly in the front yard. The moon was shining almost as bright as day and she could see a big cat up a tree in the yard. Her dogs were treeing him and he could not come down. Now Mary was not a scary person so she got her 22 rifle and put a bullet through the cat. He fell to the ground and her dogs gave him a battle to the finish. She turned the cat over to the game department. He was identified as a 'Fisher' cat found in the Everglades of Florida. Nobody knew why he was this far from home.

During the 1950's, I was on my way to Georgetown one afternoon and just below the Gumville Area, I saw a large brown cat with a long tail jump out in the center of the highway. He crouched there a few moments but as I got closer to him he made a couple of leaps and was gone. I do believe this was a panther cat.

My parents said there was a panther cat that ranged in our area in the old days. He would prowl around mostly at night making a noise which sounded like a woman screaming. My mother said it was an eerie, frightening feeling when they heard this panther holler or scream in the loneliness of a dark night.

Old Lige was deer hunting one day in the Mount Holly area. He told me he was sitting down on his deer stand when he felt like somebody was right behind him. He turned his head very slowly to see if a person had slipped up on him. To his surprise, there was a large wild cat crouched and ready to spring onto his back. He said it scared him so badly, he just swung his double barrel shotgun around next to the cat and pulled both triggers at the same time. He missed the old wild cat but managed to scare him off.

We had a few bear stories in Berkeley County to tell also. A man by the name of Slim killed a black bear down in the lower Hell Hole Swamp area, many years ago. I was told this story by a man who was there: Some men were deer hunting and the dogs got a bear moving out to the standers. He was shot and killed by Slim, who had never been much of a hunter in the first place. After the bear was killed, the men took it to a store on Highway Seventeen, north of the Cooper River.

I was told people traveling the highway would stop and look at the bear and ask a lot of questions. Slim would get very excited as he told his story of how he killed the bear.

One of the men called Packrat, decided to have some fun so he went into the store and got a jar of mustard. As Slim was telling his story, Packrat got a handful of mustard and rubbed it on the seat of Slim's pants. This really made people laugh when they saw it as they thought Ole Slim had had an accident in his pants.

After having fun for a while I was told Slim donated the bear to the game department and they had it mounted and placed on exhibit at the fair. From what I heard later, Slim's story got more and more detailed as he told it over and over throughout the years, always excluding the mustard story.

A large black bear was found dead in the early forties, coming out from Pitch Landing near Santee River below Jamestown.

Snake stories have abounded in Berkeley County. A man, by the name of Hol Cratchett, said he was hunting on a club one time and near his stand was an old car that had been abandoned years before. It started raining and Cratchett got into the dilapidated old car for shelter. A few days later, another man was on the same stand and he decided to look around the old car.

He noticed a rattlesnake inside the car and after taking a closer look, he saw several more. After the hunt was over he got some of the men together and they went to the car and began killing rattlesnakes. Old Cratchett had been extremely fortunate the day he got out of the rain. The car was home to a den of rattlesnakes. He always said he never actively went looking for trouble, so I guess that was why he missed them!

Clyde Beacon was a truck driver. I knew him well but missed seeing him for a while. When I saw him again he told me his own snake story. He needed a part for his car so he went to see a man who owned a lot of junk cars and sold used parts as a side line. He located a vehicle which would suit the occasion and got down on his stomach to look under it. Almost instantly a snake bit him in the forehead. The junk car dealer rushed him to the hospital.

The doctors began to work on him. By this time his head had swollen to an enormous size and had turned dark in color. He survived and considered he was one lucky man! Snakes love to use old cars as dens to raise their young. It is a good idea to stay away from old junk cars especially in South Carolina where the snakes are *big*!

Mac Shaeffer bought a mule from a horse trader by the name of Snuff Briggs, from Moncks Corner. This was back in the old days when transportation was hard to come by. Mac was working four twelve-hour shifts on a dredge boat at Wilson's Landing. He wanted a mule to ride home at night after getting off from work.

After his shift had ended on the dredge, he got a ride to Moncks's Corner to pick up his mule. He didn't have a saddle so he put a bridle on the mule and started riding to Shulerville bareback.

Mac rode the mule all night long! It was almost time to go back to work when he got home. He said the mule walked a leisurely pace all the way home and refused to run. Thinking the mule was hungry, Mac stopped in somebody's corn field and got him a few ears of corn. It didn't do a thing to increase the speed of that ole mule. Mac said his rear was sore as a boil when he got home, and to make matters worse, he had to go back to work without getting any sleep. As it turned out, Mac later found out the poor ole mule was just too dang old to do any running.

Chapter Twelve

I knew young Mark Chrisman well. He served as policeman in a small town of Berkeley County. One night while on duty he stopped a speeding car. The car held two of the meanest men around, even though they were from another county. The men had been to a nearby house buying a load of moonshine whiskey. Mark arrested them on the spot.

The story told to us was that young Chrisman put the law-breakers into the back seat of the car and was driving them to the Moncks Corner jail, when one of the men empted a pistol into his back. Evidently not knowing how rough the men were, Mark had not checked either of them for a gun. He died at the scene but the men responsible for his death were caught and sentenced to life in prison.

Mark Chrisman was a good person. I knew him well. He lost his life in the line of duty. This was a sad day for his family and the community.

Ole 'Stingy' Grant was eating supper one evening during the depression, with his wife Sadie. As he sat there with the wooden shutter windows open, eating cornbread and homemade syrup, in flew an ole tumblebug and landed in his plate. He picked up the bug, licked the syrup off of him and threw him out the window. "You didn't bring anything with you when you came, so by golly, you ain't taking nothing with you when you leave!" He was said to have remarked. Sadie swore it was the God's truth.

Calf Parton and his wife, Pat, were traveling 17A from Macedonia to Moncks Corner. As they began to enter highway 52 at the intersection, ole Calf asked Pat if she saw any cars coming on her side of the road. She said, "No," and Calf proceeded forward and was almost hit by an eighteen-wheeler truck. He turned to his wife, nervous and frustrated, and asked if she had seen the truck. Pat replied, "Yes, but you only asked about cars!" Talk about dumb!

Paul Johnson was working in the office of the highway department back in the ole days. There was no air conditioning and the heat was almost unbearable, so he decided to send a note to his supervisor requesting a fan. In a short while he received a note back with this message, "If you find it hot, feel free to pull off part of your clothes for there are no fans available."

Old Crick Lewis told me about the time he was raising a large type of hen chickens. An elderly neighbor woman came to his house to buy a setting of eggs so she could hatch out a batch for her own use. He said, "I'll give you the eggs but they won't hatch as I don't have a rooster." The old lady told him, "Man, if you don't have a rooster, it's a wonder those ole hens don't leave home."

Abe Willis was in the horse and mule trading business when Santee Cooper got electricity flowing down the power lines. It was a boost to his business as he could make an old mule act like a young one, by rigging up a shock wire which he would stick to the animals before he took them out on the road to sell. You can imagine the trauma of being shocked a couple of times with a hot wire or shock stick. Personally I think Abe might have benefitted by a shock or two himself just to realize how painful it was!

Old crooked Abe said he had an old mule who looked pretty good except his ears flopped back and forth when he walked. This was a sure sign of old age. Abe got some small rubber bands and rigged them up around the mule's ears next to the skin, so they were hard to see. An unsuspecting man gave Abe a good trade for the 'younger' mule, never allowing for a minute that only rubber bands stood between the old mule and youth.

Now ole Knockabout Bailey had a dapper gray horse he decided to trade to Abe for a younger one. He made the trade and after trying the new horse out for several days,

Knockabout decided he was dissatisfied and wanted Abe to bring him another one. Abe brought him a nice looking black horse and they made a trade. Abe, being the horse trader he was, always asked for extra money when he traded horses or mules. Well, even though a good bit of money had to change hands, ole Knockabout was very pleased with his new horse until the two of them got caught in a rainstorm. His black horse began to look a lot like his old gray one. To Knockabout's surprise his old horse had been dyed black and he was the owner once more, having lost a good cash in the process.

Back in the depression years of the thirties, the paper mill was built in Georgetown. Any of us boys who were big enough to pull a cross cut saw, would go into the woods and saw pulp wood for one penny per block. These pulp wood blocks were five feet long and any diameter that came into our path. We cut trees for pulpwood which would be used today for saw mill timber. It would take three or four men to put these large blocks onto the back of a truck.

This was hard, hot work. We tried to cut two hundred blocks per day which gave us five dollars a week. There was no ice water in the woods and none at home either. The coldest water we could get was by pumping an old hand pump until it brought up cool underground water.

Dab Smith lived in the Hell Hole area. Some of his family members got a job at the asbestos mill in North Charleston and moved there. During the summer months they would return for a visit. There were lots of children to feed so this old fellow began thinking how he could save on groceries when they visited. During watermelon season he would go into the field and bring in a wagon loaded with watermelons and just before his wife would ring the dinner bell, he began cutting them. By the time dinner was served, everybody had a stomach full of watermelon and there was little room left for a meal. This trick worked every time.

Now at one time ole Dab had some trouble with his neighbor. One afternoon as he was cutting firewood, the neighbor came over to settle the score. They began fighting and Dab was losing the battle even though he was sure he was doing his best. His wife walked out onto the porch about this time and as soon as he saw her watching them he came alive on his neighbor and whipped his behind but good. Dab said "There ain't no way no wife of mine is going to see me get my behind cut (whipped)!" He won the fight but he gave his wife credit for it because she was there exactly when he needed a boost!

Dab Smith was a character! One time he was hunting out of season when he was approached by a tough game warden. The warden said, "I'm going to have to take you in." Dab replied "There is only two of us here so you make your move and there will only be one of us to tell the tale." The warden decided to go back to Monck's Corner and make his report. Report made...nothing happened.

"Murder and Mayhem in Moncks Corner" was the way the headlines of the Post and Courier read after a shootout on May 4th, 1926. At the rail road crossing in Monck's Corner as a train was passing through town, three men lay dead on the depot deck.

In the late spring of 1930, Berkeley County had still more violence. On May 19th one man was killed and another wounded in an ambush at Huger Bridge (Pronounced sort of like Huge gee). On May 31st a man was shot as he was getting out of his car to enter his home in Moncks Corner. On June 3rd a man had a close call as he was driving through rural Berkeley County. On July 24th, a man was shot on main street in Moncks Corner. Thus Berkeley County became known as 'Bloody Berkeley', rivaling 'Bloody Harlan' in the coal fields of Kentucky.

The man known as the 'King Pin' of the moonshine whiskey business in Berkeley County, had a special spur track put in by the railroad, which would hold two box cars.

The railroad crew would switch out the loaded car of moonshine whiskey and replace it with an empty car as needed; in this way nothing interfered with the loading operation.

Besides the moonshine operation in Berkeley County, he had untaxed whiskey brought in from South America by the ship load. These ships would come into the area at night on high tide and were off-loaded onto small boats which then transported the whiskey to shore. The untaxed whiskey was stored in large caves with a guard on duty. His son-in-law, in later years, readily admitted the illicit actions of his wife's father.

Bill Compton told me that one day he and his brother decided to make a daring raid on the caves. They drove an old touring sedan down to the caves. When they arrived there they jumped out and started shooting all around the guard, causing him to run for his life. They loaded the car as fast as they could and left the area. Bill and his brother only did this one time as they knew their lives would be in grave danger if they risked it again. A man in the moonshine whiskey business doesn't take kindly to anyone stealing his goods.

Chapter Thirteen

On another note, a man I knew had a nice looking daughter back in the era of time when the 'hippie' movement was getting started. One night a young man with long hair came to see his daughter. The gentleman looked at the boy and asked him, "Son, is your barber dead?" The young man said, "No, sir." The irate father then made this remark, "If your barber is dead, you can use my barber, but you definitely won't be coming around here until you clean up and cut your hair!"

Arthur Dixon was arrested and charged with killing his wife. He denied doing the deed until he went on trial. When his trial started, he pleaded guilty and asked the court for mercy. His wife had a bad reputation which was brought to the attention of the judge by his lawyer. Arthur was sentenced to several years in prison but only served about eight months. When he got out of jail he went back to the company he had previously worked for, got his job back and went back to work, just as if nothing had happened.

Several years later he married a woman with four children. He said they had agreed for her mother to keep all of the children except for the baby. After the honeymoon they set up housekeeping with just one child. After a few weeks his wife brought home another one of her children to stay with them. After several more weeks, she brought home a third child. Then after another period of time, the fourth child made its' way into their home.

Arthur said, "She reminded me of an old house cat who'd move her kittens from place to place until she was satisfied with their home." It was said Arthur was good to this woman and her children, but I couldn't help but wonder what had *really* gone on between him and his first wife. I don't think anyone should become judge and jury and kill a person, for any reason.

A man I knew by the name of Potter was rough on his family. He would treat his wife mean, slap or knock his daughters around and I was told he even caused one of his daughters to be handicapped all of her life. His boy told me Potter once bought a cow in McCellanville and made him lead it all the way home, which was about thirty miles. Potter drove along in his car to keep check on him. His family did not like the way they were treated but could not do anything about it until they were grown and old enough to leave home. Potter's wife stayed with him until he died.

Boyd Hill related about the time he stopped by to visit his Uncle Ben, way out in the country. The grass in the old man's yard was about knee high but Uncle Ben was sitting out on the porch with a nice breeze blowing, not a worry in the world. Boyd asked him, casual like, "When are you going to cut your grass, Uncle?" Ben replied, "I'm waiting on the grass to seed out and then I'm going to let the chickens eat the seed. Saves a body time and money that way!" Reminded me of the time when a friend brought a chicken into the house to eat the watermelon seeds out of the watermelon for him. His wife about killed him after cleaning up chicken manure and seeds from all over the place!

Tate Wilson stopped by Charlie Mann's house one day to buy a bunch of collards. Ole Charlie was sitting on the porch doing nothing. While he went to get the collards, Tate sat in his car. When Charlie came back from the garden, Tate told him, "While I was sitting here I could hear your water pump running. It's water logged but I can tell you how to fix it if you want me to." Ole Charlie replied, "I know what's wrong with it, I just ain't felt like fixing it!"

Matt Hildebrande lived near the church parsonage and since he owned the land next to it he had always given the pastor a place to plant a garden. But the church happened to get a pastor Matt simply didn't like. Matt told me his one desire was to catch the preacher away from the church so he could see who the better man happened to be.

As time went on, Matt kept thinking of ways he could harass the preacher. The preacher had a nice fall garden planted with some pretty collards he anticipated enjoying during the winter. Matt hired one of his neighbors with a tractor to plow everything up. He owned the land so there was nothing the preacher could do about it.

Ole Matt had a horse he allowed to graze on the land adjacent to the parsonage. The preacher had a dog that would run Matt's horse around the pasture anytime he took a notion.

One day I stopped by to visit Matt and he was sitting on the porch with a double barrel shotgun across his lap. Being summer time, I asked him what he planned to hunt or to shoot. He said, "I'm tired of the preacher's dog running my horse so I'm just waiting for him to try it today."

I talked with him for a while and tried to convince him not to harm the dog. A few days later, I got word the dog had sneaked back into Matt's pasture and started running his horse. It was the last time, for the ill fated mutt met with a load of buckshot.

Blake Rodman worked as a salesman and his territory covered several southern states. He was down in Tennessee and the highways were not familiar to him. He took an unfamiliar road and realized he was headed in the wrong direction. Blake didn't see any patrol cars so he cut across the median and took off the other way.

Just a few miles down the highway, a patrol car pulled up beside him. The officer inside it motioned with his hand for Blake to pull over to the shoulder of the road. The patrolman got out of his car and walked up to Blake and asked him, "Son, where are you from?" Blake replied, I was born and reared in Berkeley County, South Carolina. I'm on my way to Nashville to make a record." The patrolman told him, "I want you to head on back to South

Carolina. If I ever see you again, you will be making a record but it will be doing time in a Tennessee jail."

Carl Temperman says he once trapped a wildcat and decided to have some fun with it. He got a large cardboard box and with much difficulty, managed to get the wildcat inside it. He then took some rope and tied it around the box to secure it. It was Saturday afternoon and traffic around Moncks Corner was pretty heavy. When Carl got a chance, he ran out into the middle of the highway and set the box down. He ran back onto the edge of the road and got behind some bushes.

Along came a carload of people and they stopped, picked up the box with the wildcat in it and put it on the back seat. They started up the highway and had gone just a short distance when Carl saw them stop the car and all four doors fly open. They had opened the box and the wildcat jumped out. They gave it plenty of leeway to escape and the furious animal headed for the woods. Carl said that he still laughs when he thinks about it.

Ole Ira Jones didn't want to go into the service during World War II. He loved things just as they were so he got to thinking how he could avoid the draft. He finally decided to shoot his trigger finger off. It worked and he was turned down at Fort Jackson. His brother decided to do the same thing and he, too, was turned down. They both spent the war-time making good corn whiskey, but Ira got caught. Unfortunately his missing finger didn't keep him from serving time in jail.

Ray Liberman told me he always wanted to be a barber in Moncks Corner in the old days. He finally managed to get some tools and was hired into a shop. He didn't know a thing about cutting hair but figured surely he could learn on the job. Just a few days after he began working at the local shop, right at closing time, several men came in and told him he was no longer welcome.

They closed in around him and he stepped behind his chair with a straight razor in his hand. He said to them, "I can't get all of you but the first one that comes on me will get his throat cut!" They didn't push the issue any further so he took his tools with him when he left the shop shortly afterwards. He said the handwriting was on the wall, "I knew I would not be able to work in peace there." He began his journey up north. He worked in any shop that would hire him until the owner found out he wasn't too good at the barber profession. He managed to work a few days at each shop until he learned the trade. He ended up in Washington D.C. where he married and made quite a bit of money. He would buy a barber shop, get a good business going and then sell it at a nice profit. He also worked with real estate and made a small fortune.

After retiring he moved back to Berkeley County and bought a nice tract of land with a home on it. He fenced up part of the land and started buying and selling cows. He enjoyed going to the market and always dressed in a silk shirt, white hat and alligator shoes.

I overheard two old men talking about him at the market one day. One man asked the other, "Who is that old man who comes to the market dressed so sporty?" The other man said, "They tell me that he is an ole Berkeley County boy that went up north and really showed them Yanks a thing or two!" Actually, I think he showed the men who ran him out of Berkeley County, a thing or two also.

Macedonia high school was burned to the ground after graduation exercises in 1938. A friend of mine graduated that night and he quickly informed me that he was home in bed when his family got word the school house was on fire.

Macedonia high school burned again before daylight on August 4th, 1996. According to the News & Courier, a deputy sheriff was patrolling the area when he saw the fire. He sounded the alarm and all the fire departments near Macedonia came to help put out the fire. The fire departments are to be commended as they were able to save the other structures. We lost the old high school from which I graduated in 1941. The first class to graduate from the new school was the class of 1940. Since there were no facilities for graduation exercises in 1939, they had to graduate along with the class of 1940, although their diplomas and class rings gave the year '1939'.

Alvin Nader was from another county but every Sunday he drove his father over to Berkeley County to preach at the old Baptist church. This was in the late thirties. A Berkeley County boy by the name of Whip Jackson, decided he was going to beat up on Alvin, so he began to map out his strategy. He took an old spring off a screen door, melted lead and poured it on one end of the spring until he got a nice chunk hanging from it. Then Whip took a chamois string and attached it to the other end so it would fit around his wrist. This string was supposed to help him hold onto his homemade Blackjack when he started hitting Alvin with it.

Sunday night came and Whip was ready for his fight. He invited Alvin down the road a short distance from the church, so they could have their fight in peace. As they walked down the road in the darkness, ole Whip made a quick pass at Alvin with his home-made Blackjack, hitting Alvin on the head. Alvin was dazed for a few moments but when he got his wits together, he put a whipping on the Berkeley County boy, ole Whip Jackson. The next day we checked the area where they fought and found the home-made Blackjack. We kept it as a souvenir for quite a while. It is amazing the effort men will put into for a fight!

A young man by the name of Will Martin decided to go squirrel hunting one day in the late summer. He picked up his 22 rifle and went up to the swamp in front of his house. He saw a squirrel, shot it and when it fell to the ground, unbeknownst to Will, it fell near a large rattlesnake. Will walked over to where the squirrel lay, dead as a door-nail.

As he reached down to pick it up the distraught rattle-snake, struck him on the back of his hand.

When Will realized he was snake bit, he threw his rifle down and ran home. Running caused the venom to spread faster throughout his body. When he got home his uncle wanted to cut and bleed the fang marks. Will said 'no', he wanted to get to the doctor's right away. There was no car available so again he ran, this time out to the highway to hitch-hike a ride. A lady came along and took him to the doctor's office in St. Stephens. They rushed him to the Berkeley County hospital. The doctor knew it was a large snake due to the width of the fang marks. They did all they could to save his life, but to no avail. After enduring a lot of pain, Will passed away during the night. I knew this young man well and I have thought about this incident many times. Some of the family members looked for the rifle but to my knowledge no one ever found it. I guess the falling leaves shrouded it the first winter and each passing year just added more cover to the missing rifle.

Paul Richmond loved to drink moonshine whiskey back during the depression years, when the bootleggers still made good whiskey. They used upright copper distilleries with oak barrels to set up their mash. This whiskey smelled good and tasted good. I saw Paul many times, walking the old country roads with a quart jar of corn whiskey in his hand. He would stop when he felt like it, take a swig or two, and usually pass out on a ditch bank.

One day he made it to the old country store. The lady who ran the store bought eggs from the local farmers or she would accept eggs in exchange for groceries. She kept them in a box behind the counter. Paul, being drunk and very hungry, crawled behind the counter, took out his pocket knife and began to knock holes in the eggs and drink the contents. He had the floor littered with egg shells, before the store-owner caught him. She got a broom and began hitting him until he crawled out from behind the counter and out the door. The store-owner called after him, "Don't ever let me catch you in here again as you are nothing but a suck-egg dog!"

I saw Paul several years later and he informed me he had quit drinking. He told me one Sunday morning after his family left for church he took his jar of whiskey, set it up on a gate post and shot it to pieces with his shotgun. He said, "Whiskey made a fool out of me for the last time." He made up his mind and never took another drink. 'Ole Suck-egg' became a respected man in his community.

This story made the pages of a true detective magazine in 1945. It told the story of two Berkeley County boys, hitchhiking. They were given a ride by a salesman. Nobody knew exactly what happened but one of the boys was later caught with the salesman's body in the trunk of the car. His girlfriend turned him over to the law. The young man spent many years in prison. He was finally pardoned and came back to his hometown area to live. I met him after he got out of prison and always enjoyed talking with him. He really had some tales to tell about the chain gangs. I knew all of his family and they were good people.

One of his sister's-in-law told me he came to their house one night and stayed very late. He discussed his time in prison and the crime he was accused of committing. He told his family he was falsely accused. He swore he had not killed the salesman. Of course we all know there have been times when the wrong person was put in prison. But I guess no one will ever know for sure if this young man was guilty or innocent. It's entirely possible though, he had convinced himself over the years, that he had not committed the gruesome crime.

Chapter Fourteen

Carl Penny was in the bootleg whiskey business. He was good at his trade and never was caught until someone reported him to the IRS. He liked to ride his horse to his whiskey still as the horse was fast transportation when the law moved in on him. The horse also served as a watch 'dog'.

When operating his moonshine distillery, he would tie his horse nearby and keep an eye on it, as a horse can pick up movements in the bushes a human cannot. When a horse spots something in a distance they will look in that direction with their ears pointed forward.

He told me of one particular time when he was a bit careless and his horse was looking at something before he realized it. He ran to his horse, jumped on its' back and left in a hurry. The lawmen were almost on him and began to shoot all around him. He could hear the bullets hitting the trees. The revenuers tore up his still but he got away.

During World War II another man went into business with Carl. They made big money even though sugar and jars were hard to come by. They finally had to turn to the black market to get these items and they were expensive. In later years Carl changed his lifestyle and operated a legitimate business, bought, no doubt, by moonshine money.

A man I knew by the name of Truman, started a small café in a little town in Berkeley County during World War II. When the young men, myself included, began returning home from service, this became a meeting place for us. There was always a side show in the café if you stayed long enough. There were plenty of fights, a few stray women, and of course the law always trying to lock somebody up. Truman was a tough character and kept his blackjack and 38 pistol ready at all times. He was known to have beat up several people with his blackjack when they started trouble in his café. One night after closing, some men decided to show him a trick or two. They circled his café and riddled it with bullets. Luckily no one was hurt. To my knowledge the perpetrators were never taken to court.

One night, Hoit Smith, a local policeman, was in the café when Bill Burnham, who was known to be a rough customer, knocked him to the floor. Bill then humbly apologized, saying he thought Hoit was a fireman since he had on a blue uniform.

Back in those days, most all the fellows had a jar of moonshine in their car, although beer was served at most 'road houses'. Sometimes we shared our corn whiskey with the local law officers if we knew them well enough.

One night, two law officers were on hand to break up a disturbance at the little café. They were driving a four door car. As soon as they would arrest one man and put him in the back seat and go to make another arrest, their prisoner would slip out the other car door and mingle with the spectators. I had to wonder about the intelligence of the officers and for that reason, I figured it best not to mention their names!

This little café made history for a while but as the years went by, things changed and a young man, Zeke Templeton, was shot and killed there. I think this was about the last round-up. I suspect the women folk in our lives were not saddened to see it go!

Bill White told me of the circumstances which actually took place at a church in Berkeley County. He had a friend who was there and the newspaper also carried the story.

The church only had one door, which was the front door. The preacher was behind the pulpit when the congregation was asked to stand while they passed the collection plate to take up tithes and offerings.

Clyde Wentworth, a rough man if there ever was one, was having trouble with a church member and had come looking for him with a gun. As he arrived and looked in the door, he saw the man he was looking for, right out in the aisle shouting up a storm, obviously consumed with righteousness! Clyde stood at the door and fired his gun at the whooping church member. He almost shot the preacher. The preacher ran down the aisle to the front door, jumped over the steps, and into the church yard. A man was standing outside near the steps and swore he heard the preacher make this remark, "I'll *never* preach another sermon in a one door church!"

Art Ellie loved to make and haul corn whiskey. He also was fond of hunting and fishing and he was as good at one as the other. He really loved to turkey hunt in the spring and could call a gobbler up to him without any trouble. One day he invited a couple of men to go fishing with him and he told them not to bring any fishing gear. *He* preferred to catch fish the *easy* way.

As darkness settled, the two men met Art at the landing where he had his boat. They started paddling up the river a short distance when Art hung a light on the side of the boat next to the bank. As he paddled along the edge of the river where the fish were feeding, the fish would get scared and start jumping out of the water. Some of the frightened fish would fall into the boat. The light would either blind them or attract them as they were hemmed in alongside the boat. I have never personally tried this but I have been told that it works. I suspect it works better if one has had a swig or two of moonshine!

Arizona Cole went to town for a visit with some friends on a particular day and he came home around midnight. His wife had already gone to bed, but he insisted she get up and fix him some supper. They had an argument and he threatened to shoot her. He reached up and got his shotgun out of the gun rack. He kept his gun loaded and she knew it, so, fearful for her life, she tried to get the gun from him. As they began fighting for control of the shotgun, it fired accidently. The load of shot cut the main artery in his leg. His wife quickly rushed Arizona to the hospital but he didn't make it.

To the best of my knowledge, it was ruled an accident. I don't know if his widow married again, but if she did, you can be sure her man didn't try to force her to cook him a meal in the middle of the night!

Dr. Porter was a dentist with an office in one of the small towns in Berkeley County. He was up in age and had told a number of people about having a ringing in his ears which would not go away. He sought medical help but could not get any relief. One day someone passing by his office saw him lying back in his dental chair as though he was asleep. Truth was he had taken a straight razor and cut his own throat. This was a very sad day.

Brick Halsy had come to Berkeley County from another part of the state. He loved to hunt and went along with us every chance he got. We were hunting on the Tiger Corner Road and I left him on the first stand as I walked the bank to get to my own stand. We put a man out to drive with his pack of dogs from the Jamestown side of us. We had another man driving from the Tiger Corner side. The dogs on the Jamestown side jumped a deer and were heading toward us. The other dogs had not struck trail yet, so they started for the dogs that were already running. As they passed by, Halsy shot into the bushes thinking they were deer.

I knew what had happened the minute I heard the dogs howling. I went back to Halsy and as I got close to him, I could see him kneeling down. Sure enough he had hit some of the dogs with buckshot. He was very upset and brokenly told me, "Let's get these dogs to a veterinarian and I'll pay the bill."

One of the dogs was mine and I took him to the vet. Nothing could save him though, since he had been shot full force in the head. The other dog lived but since she had buckshot through her hip and leg she was handicapped for the rest of her life. When the game warden heard about this episode he asked if we wanted to press charges. The warden said, "I can charge him the same as if he had shot a doe deer. We know he was not looking for horns!" He went on to say truthfully, "Any man who would shoot into the bushes without seeing his target clearly, should have to pay a big fine! It's a good thing it wasn't a man in them bushes!" We asked the warden to let it go as an accident since Halsy was our friend and we *hoped* he had learned a lesson.

We have had several people shot in Berkeley County in hunting accidents, because the hunter got over-excited and shot at the first movement he saw in the bushes! I am a victim myself as I caught two buck-shots when a deer ran between me and another stander. The hunter emptied his shotgun in a fury to kill the deer. I could have been killed! I try to watch who I take a stand by after that incident.

Del Kane was getting up in age but he still liked to deer hunt. One day he was sitting on a stool up an old dirt road, waiting for a deer to come by. A young man by the name of Whit, was driving by in his pickup with a high powered rifle, looking for a deer or a wild hog to shoot. As he passed the road, he saw old man Kane on his stool and thought it was an animal. Whit got his rifle, pulled a bead on the object and pulled the trigger. To his surprise a man jumped straight up with his arms in the air and fell face forward on the ground. Whit rushed Mr. Kane to the hospital but he died several days later.

Cal Dennis was well known in the old days, when most people were using mules and wagons for transportation. He lived near a church which frequently held revivals lasting two or three weeks. There were times when folks would come a long distance and they would want to spend the night with Cal. I was told he would meet his guests out front, call one of his boys and tell him to unhook the man's mule, put him in the stable and give him twelve ears of corn. By his side he would hold out three or four fingers. This would be the number of ears of corn he really wanted his son to give the animal. Old Cal was something else!

Some friends of mine were deer hunting on the Sabbath in the ole days when their dogs jumped a white deer and ran it by the standers. Having never seen a white deer, they let it go by without shooting it. After the drive was over, they got together and decided to go home and quit hunting on Sunday. They figured the Lord had sent the white deer out to them as a reminder that it was the Sabbath day and they should not be hunting. I have seen Albino deer in this state on a few occasions. I feel sure this was the situation with them but it was enough to stop them from hunting on Sunday.

Hap Morris came from upstate as a young man and got a job with a wholesale company out of Charleston. On his first day he was sent to deliver beer to a rough joint in Berkeley County. As he walked in the door of the dive, some fellows began shooting up the place. The bullets were flying around him as he ducked out the door and headed back to Charleston. Hap told his boss, "If you want beer delivered to that joint, you can carry it yourself! I'll be damned if I am going back there again!"

Darcy Mattson told me of the time when he was out of work and barely getting by, although he did run a little moonshine whiskey now and then. A friend told Darcy he and his family were coming to visit for Sunday dinner. Back then people didn't wait for an invitation to visit, the way they do now. If they saw you out somewhere they might tell you of their plans, but then again, they might just show up about meal time. Darcy said when he went to bed on Saturday night, he was aware they had nothing to cook for Sunday dinner. Along about daylight Sunday morning, he was awakened by the sound of ducks feeding in a pond near his house. It was winter so he jumped out of bed, dressed warmly, got his shotgun and headed to the pond.

As Darcy got near the pond, the ducks saw him and started flying away. Darcy fixed both barrels into the ducks and several hit the water. He picked them up and headed for home, where he informed his wife to put on a pot of rice! They were going to have rice and gravy with roast duck for dinner!

The family visiting with Darcy were church going people so he didn't bother to tell them they were eating ducks killed out of season on a Sabbath morning. Darcy always got a good laugh when telling this story.

Bob Still operated a small business in Berkeley County. I don't know all the circumstances but early one morning his house was set afire. He jumped up, got his money box and started running to his neighbor's house. As he ran, a man caught up with him and cut him severely. Bob died at the scene.

I was told Bob kept a pistol near his money box, but he was in such a hurry to get away from the fire that he inadvertently left it in the house. Had he taken a short moment to pick up his pistol the story would be different. Bob was a good shot and could easily have killed or maimed his assailant, thus saving his own life. Such tragedies were almost common-place in Berkeley County, South Carolina.

Chapter Fifteen

Reggie Holland told me he was old enough to know all about the stock market crash in 1929. The banks closed up and a lot of people lost their money. People didn't trust banks after that so they began hoarding their money and keeping it out of circulation, thus causing a depression. The president decided to call in all the old money and replace it with new currency. The people had to bring in their hoarded and obsolete money to exchange for the new bills. These new bills are the same as we carry in our wallets today. This smart move may have been instrumental in helping get the country moving again.

Ole Gabby loved to ride over to Lake Moultrie and look for trot lines. When he found a good full line, he would take the fish and move on. It didn't matter to Gabby that he had nearly gotten shot by a man with a high powered rifle who caught Gabby in the act. Gabby kept it up like nothing had ever happened. Due to numerous reports of his illegal fishing, the game warden began watching the lake more closely. They finally caught Gabby. As a result he was taken into court and had to pay a large fine. The thing that made the fishermen happy was that ole Gabby was barred from fishing on the lake anymore.

Phil Baker was using a large piece of equipment to cut a ditch in Berkeley County. He went home for the weekend and Monday morning found him back on the job. To his surprise someone had stolen his tools, oil and grease. He went to see the magistrate and the magistrate passed the problem on to the constable.

The constable investigated the situation for a few days and came back to the magistrate with this story, "I don't have any leads and I don't have a man in my mind to lay it on."

Ole 'Gator Creech loved to hunt alligators and was very good at it. Along with his buddy, they would go into the river at night with their boat, shine a light in the eyes of the alligators and shoot them with a high powered rifle. One of the men would then jump out of the boat, get hold of the alligator and pull him into the boat before the old gator went down. This was dangerous but it was a sure way to make money. I knew Gator well and he was not afraid to tackle an alligator. In the old days he could get a dollar per foot for the hide. 'Gator and his friend would cut the tails off the alligators and put them in a freezer until they got a large number of them. They would then take the meat to a man who operated a store and had an electric meat saw. Working together they could slice up the alligator tails in a short while.

I was there one day when they had finished cutting up a bunch of alligator tails and fried some for dinner. I tried them. They were extremely good. I heard tell they sell at a high price today. Now only designated people are allowed to kill an alligator in South Carolina since they are regulated by the state.

Eric Smalls said that when he was a teenager, and the oldest, in a large family, he didn't have shoes and the weather was getting cold. It was during the early part of World War II and his father had gotten a job somewhere in the north area.

This particular night his father came home from work with one pair of shoes. The children were all hunkered down in front of the fireplace trying to stay warm. The father threw the shoes in the midst of the children and said that whoever they fit could have them.

Eric said he managed to take the sought after shoes from the other children and began trying them on, but they were too tight. He knew he couldn't wear them but he was not about to give them up! He began thinking how he could stretch them. Being a country boy, he was aware dried cowpeas would swell if you left them in water overnight. Most people on a farm had cow peas, so he filled both of the shoes with them and put water on them overnight. The cowpeas swelled up, stretching his shoes so that when he dumped them the next day, he was able to put on his shoes and walk off. Eric was a lucky fellow to have shoes to wear, through sheer ingenuity. I think 'sheer ingenuity' brought us all through the hardest of times.

Chris Aldridge told us how in the old days of open range, people's cows were allowed to run loose in the woods and had to be dipped to control ticks. The cows were rounded up by men on horseback, using dogs to help them. Concrete vats were filled with water with the necessary medicine mixed into it. Holding pens were built for the cows to be driven into before they were put into the vats to be dipped. They were then made to jump into the deep vat and swim to the other side, thereby covering their entire body with the treated water. Next, they would go into a drip pen where they would be held for a short time in order for the treated water to run back into the vat, thereby saving water and medicine. Someone would then dab a spot of paint on each one of them before they let the confused, but tick free, cows out. The bright paint would show the owners which cows had been treated against the freeloading ticks.

Sometime in the late forties, the law was changed concerning open range and it was reversed to 'closed', which is the way it now stands today.

Greg Harwick reported that he joined the navy to see the world. He has seen the world and now wants to know how to get out.

Back in the fifties a politician friend of mine, Gus Whitley, told me that he had always wanted to have his family history traced but could not afford it, as it was quite expensive. Gus said however, that when he decided to run for public office his opponent took care of it for him and he didn't have to spend a dime. This is known today as being good politics.

A gentleman friend, Mason More, was fifty years old and one day he told his buddy, Cap Lang, that he would like to meet a woman of the same age with no bad habits. Cap replied, "I'm looking for the same woman, Mason. If you find her, please advise me of the location. I would love to meet her."

Sue Miller said she was tired of living near so many Brown's so she left Berkeley County. She rode the Grey Hound bus to Lake City, South Carolina. As she got off the bus and looked around, one of the first buildings she saw had a sign over the top that read, 'Brown Manufacturing Co.' In anguish Sue told the bus driver, "My Lord, here's where they manufacture the Browns! Wait for me! I'm moving on!"

Two brothers, Clyde and Luke, had an argument and decided to settle it with their shotguns. Luke ran behind the first tree he saw, toting his trusty shotgun with him. Clyde found himself a big tree and got behind it. As they began to look for a good shot at each other, Luke's arm stuck out from behind his tree and Clyde shot it off! Of course Clyde took Luke to the hospital and saved his life, but Luke had to go through life with only one arm, a reminder to both of them of sibling foolishness. Clyde and Luke were good rugged individuals and I hunted and fished with them many times. They both considered the accident, 'the foolishness of youth.'

A well-to-do business man from a small town in Berkeley County, by the name of Avery Halcomb, noted to his friend that his mother, Sarah-Beth, was one smart woman. When his friend asked why, he pointed out to him. "See how mother is sitting in that chair near the highway on this hot day? Well, as the traffic flows along the highway the air current is moved toward her. This is keeping her cool and she doesn't have to run her air conditioner in the house. This saves her money." Now that is being frugal! They say she died a millionaire.

Casey Freedman was a tall, heavy set man who owned a small farm in Berkeley County. Most folks wouldn't tangle with Casey, because of his size and strength. Due to an argument over some trivial misdeed or the other Casey had to fight three brothers at one time. He knocked one of them unconscious as the fight began but another one was hitting him in the back. He told him "keep pecking, little man and I'll take care of you in just a minute." At that moment the third brother ran into Casey with a knife and cut his stomach open. This really made Casey angry! He whipped all three of them but lost a lot of blood before having to walk to the doctor's office. The doctor did his best but could not save him.

Old Bluenose swore he would not eat catfish. When asked why he replied, "Catfish are the devil's own! Look at them horns hanging down from their heads! Why, if I et one of them suckers, I would feel like I was eatin' dinner with the devil!"

A man by the name of Carson, who later became a good friend of mine, was working in Wadboo Swamp with a logging company, back in the twenties. They had to use a two-man cross cut saw along with the ole axe. It was hard work, hot in the swamp in the summer and cold in the winter. Carson had taken about all he could stand physically and he figured there had to be a better way to make a living somewhere in this country.

One morning he went to work and decided it was time to quit. He stuck his axe in a tree stump and left it there and walked away toward Charleston. There he joined the navy and spent over twenty years sailing the oceans without coming home.

I met Carson after World War II had ended. I had known some of his people but had never heard of him. He came back to Berkeley County after being discharged from the navy. I asked him how he had managed to stay away for over twenty years without coming back to visit his family, especially his mother. His answer was "I knew if I came home I would never go back. I wanted to make at least twenty years in the navy to get a pension for life." He made his time and got his pension. Carson was a good man and I will never forget the days we spent fishing on the river together or the fish fries we had on the river bank with our friends. That was about fifty years ago and life was not in the fast lane back then. We took time to enjoy our family and friends as television had not come onto the scene at that time.

El Bishop had a job during the fifties making about $150.00 per week. He had to drive to North Charleston every day from Shulerville. He started thinking about this situation and decided he could make just as much money at home with his two barrel moonshine distillery. He could tend his farm while waiting on the mash to ferment.

He quit his job and stayed home, made whiskey, and ran his farm. His carefree lifestyle must have agreed with him for ole El is now in his eighties and still driving his car.

McCall Preston informed me that he used to work with the Revenue agents, locating and breaking up illegal moonshine operations. He also told me he had a picture of Al Capone standing near cases upon cases of moonshine whiskey stacked near a dirt road in Berkeley County, ready to be loaded and hauled away. It was a known fact that Al Capone was in Berkeley County on several occasions.

Rush Clark was a land surveyor. He told me about a church in Berkeley County that was having problems and could not agree on the land situation. He was hired to make a survey and establish the boundary lines.

One morning Rush got his crew and headed there to make the survey. In just a short while a lady by the name of Mercy, came upon them with her shotgun, demanding they leave or she would shoot. Rush didn't want any trouble so he took his men back to Moncks Corner and told the sheriff his problem. The sheriff designated a deputy to go with them for protection until they could get the survey made.

Later on the same church hired a man who owned a tree service to cut the limbs from some trees around the cemetery. He later told me that he was up in a tree cutting limbs when he heard someone hollering on the ground beneath him. He cut off his power saw to hear what was being said and there was Mercy with her shotgun. She told him to come down or she would shoot him down.

He said that he didn't want to get shot so he came down, loaded up his equipment and went home. He didn't bother to go back.

Speaking of churches, Ed Morris told me that he went down to a little church in the Hellhole area looking for a girl friend. He saw this good looking young lady by the name of Lisa and decided he would like to have her as his wife. He made conversation with her and she was pleasant to talk with, so he figured he had made it to first base. He then got up the nerve to ask to take her home after church. She agreed. Some of the Hell hole boys decided they didn't like Ed dating their pretty Lisa, so they began pulling tricks on him. These boys collected some sand spurs and while Ed and Lisa were in church, they scattered them on both seats of Ed's car. After church was over the couple came out and got into the car to go home. The sand spurs began sticking them and they had to get out of the car and clean the seats before they could go any further. At this point they were not suspicious of any wrong-doing.

Shortly after that, again while they were in church, the boys picked up the rear end of Ed's car and blocked it up so the wheels could not touch the ground. As Ed tried to drive away with his Lisa, the wheels would only spin. He and Lisa finally had to get help before they could move the car. By this time Ed realized somebody was out to get him, and he was on his guard. That didn't stop the boys from pulling another trick when they chocked the wheels so the car couldn't pull. None of the tricks worked however and it must have been true love for the couple did get married.

Old Dale Weeks drove his mule and wagon to church in the old days. One Sunday night some boys decided to swap his front wheels with his rear wheels, which are quite a bit larger. The old gentleman and his family were traveling in the dark on their way home when he looked over at his wife and remarked, "It appears to me that we are going uphill all the time!"

Two brothers, Clarence and Nathan, owned land joining each other with a line fence between them. One day Clarence's hogs got over into Nathan's corn field and were having a picnic. Nathan sent one of his boy's over to inform his brother. Clarence sent this message back, "Tell your daddy that I have never seen corn hurt a hog yet. Just tell him to let them eat all the corn they want and don't worry himself none!"

Ollie was having a hard time trying to make a living for his family in the ole days. He kept a small stock of chickens on his farm to supply his family with eggs and sometimes he would butcher a chicken for the table. He started missing some of his chickens and had suspicions as to what was happening to them. After deciding on a culprit, he approached Bull Simpson and told him, "Mister, I believe you have been stealing my chickens!" Bull replied, "No sir, I don't steal and there's no way I would bother you *or* your chickens."

Ollie decided to rig up a trap gun in his chicken house and this way he could be sure who was stealing from him. He mounted the gun in the chicken house so that it would discharge about knee high. Then he tied a string to the trigger, rigging it up so that it would pull the trigger as the door to the chicken house was opened. Sometime during the night, the gun went off. Ollie jumped out of bed and went out to see who had been shot but to his surprise the man was gone, leaving a trail of blood.

Meanwhile Bull came down with a mysterious illness and went to live with his sister and brother-in-law who lived nearby. He stayed with them until he was feeling better and then he went home. Word got out about the shooting. Ollie had no more problems with his chickens.

Ed Marcell was having a problem with someone stealing corn out of his barn. He put a heavy lock on the door. To his surprise the corn kept disappearing although the lock was not broken. After inspecting his barn closely he found some boards which were not nailed as tight as they should be. He figured someone was slipping the boards off at night, reaching through the open spaces and stealing the corn without going through the door. He bought some steel traps used to catch animals and placed them around the wall, inside the barn. Each trap had a chain on it to secure it to the inside wall.

One morning Ed got up to check his traps and there was his neighbor, ole Hitch Martin, standing by the barn with his hand caught in a trap. There was no way he could get his hand out of the trap or get the trap loose as it was nailed to the wall. Hitch had been removing a couple of boards, reaching through the opening and filling his bags with corn. Ed solved his problem although it was very embarrassing to ole Hitch.

Ole Clyde loved to fight and would accommodate anybody who wanted to have a little physical contact. He was a veteran of World War I and had been trained to operate in close contact.

It was a few days before Christmas in the late thirties when his two daughters were at the nearby church practicing for a Christmas program. Two of Clyde's teen-age brothers-in-law were riding around drinking moonshine whiskey out of a two quart fruit jar. They stopped in front of the church and decided to take a drink. As they sat there, along came two tough older guys by the names of Will and Frank, looking for trouble. Will and Frank started an argument and with all four of them slightly drunk, there was a fight. After trading licks for a few minutes, Will and Frank won the fight. About this time one of the daughters ran next door to the general store where her father was trading and told him the story. Clyde came running to the church and started fighting with Will and Frank. He knocked Frank down, jumped on him and pushed his fingers into his eyes, popping them out of the sockets. This ended the fight as Frank had to be taken to the hospital to have his eyes put back in their sockets. We saw Frank, eyes bandaged and all, a couple of days later with Will driving him around town. I reckon Will and Frank weren't so tough after that incident!

Frank recovered from the episode and in later years moved to Florida to make his home. Old Clyde told me that he had done this before to his lieutenant in World War I. He and the lieutenant could not get along so one day the lieutenant told Clyde to meet him on this little hill behind the barracks, when the ranks were dismissed.

When the day's training ended, Clyde told me that he ran to the top of a hill and was ready for the lieutenant when he got there. They began fighting and he was having a hard battle until they went to the ground. He then pushed his fingers into the lieutenant's eyes until they popped out of their sockets. This ended the fight and Clyde called for help to get the lieutenant to the hospital. There was never a court martial and Clyde received no set-downs from the army. Needless to say, Clyde didn't have any more problems with the lieutenant either.

Art Cain was having problems with his neighbor, Bob Halsey. One day Art saw Bob driving his horse and buggy on the dirt road that passed near Art's house. Art ran outside and hid behind a shed near the road until his neighbor passed by. He then ran and jumped into the back of the buggy as it was moving along. Art knocked Bob out of the buggy and they fell to the ground. As they were fighting the ole horse kept on going with the empty buggy.

Someone caught the horse later and returned her to Bob. The magistrate put both Art and Bob under a peace bond. This helped them to respect each other although they did have a couple of small incidents later.

Chapter Sixteen

Jim Priest loved to smoke cigars. One Christmas day he had been outside with his grandchildren shooting cherry bombs, a powerful and dangerous type of fire works. His wife called them inside for dinner and Jim put the remaining cherry bombs in his shirt pocket. After eating a large Christmas dinner, he went into the living room and laid back in his favorite recliner. He lit a cigar and in a few minutes he fell asleep with the cigar still in his mouth. As Jim slept the lit end of the cigar fell down into his shirt pocket, lighting off the cherry bombs. There was a loud explosion and Jim fell out of the chair onto the floor.

His wife, Sue, ran into the living room to see her husband lying in the floor and not breathing. She began CPR on him until he began breathing again. He survived but said he learned a valuable lesson that day and would never carry fireworks in his pocket again.

Marsh Fallwell was getting up in age and lived by himself. His brother, Nash, checked on him regularly to see that he was ok. Marsh's house did not have indoor plumbing so when nature called one cold winter day, he had to make the long walk to the outdoor privy. While sitting in the cold outhouse, Marsh suffered a stroke which partially paralyzed his body. He could not get up and as night came on, the weather began to get very cold. The stroke did not affect his mind to the degree that he could not use common sense, so Marsh began to wonder what he could do to keep warm. Being a deer hunter, he kept a couple of deer dogs running loose in the yard. He began calling his dogs and finally one came to him. With waning strength, he took the dog in his lap, wrapped his arms around him and stayed in that position until the next day. When Nash came by to check on Marsh and could not find him in the house, he began looking outside. He located Marsh and his dog in the outhouse and took him to the hospital.

Marsh stayed in the hospital several days and was then taken to a nursing home where he lived for many years. He was in his eighties when he passed away. I knew Marsh all of my life and he was a rugged individual. He made and sold some of the best moonshine whiskey in the county. It was crystal clear with a good taste and smell. He used all copper with cypress board containers to ferment his mash.

A widow lady by the name of Martha, had three nice looking daughters. They lived in my neighborhood and I knew them well. They could all play the piano, as well as sing. On Sunday afternoons they usually played and sang to entertain people who came by to visit them.

One Sunday afternoon ole Dag Hamrick came by to hear them sing. He thought he was right proper with his speech and often used big words, while completely oblivious of their meaning. This day as the crowd was gathering to hear the girls play and sing, ole Dag decided he would show them how well he could express himself. He called Martha to his side and gave her this request, "Would you and your lovely daughters please urinate on the piano for us?!?" Martha was gracious about it although everyone else was doubled with laughter. Old Dag never did realize the laugh was on him.

Grant Hill was a caretaker on a large plantation in Berkeley County. Evening time always found him on the job, riding his horse and looking for people night hunting on the property. Grant always carried a double barrel shotgun with him. This night he rode up on three men who were walking and shining lights for deer. When these men saw him they hid their guns in the bushes, denying they were night hunting. They began arguing with the caretaker. Grant told them, "There are three of you and I only have this double barrel shotgun but I can guarantee you that if you push me, two of you will die tonight and if I can reload fast enough, I will get all of you!" The men decided not to push the issue and walked out of the woods ahead of Grant. He took them to the local sheriff and they were arrested.

Bill Spurlock had a mule with a problem. It was summer time and his mule was covered with sores. I stopped by his house one day and he had the mule tied to a tree with burnt motor oil spread all over its' body. The hot sun was shining on the mule and he was very uncomfortable. We were discussing the problem when Bill's wife came to the door and voiced her opinion, "I told my husband to sell the mule! There is bound to be a sucker out there somewhere! My husband might be the head of the house but I am the neck and the neck turns the head." I guess that meant she was the boss. Sure enough someone bought the mule.

Flint Macall was up in age and living alone. He didn't give it a thought when two men came to his house telling him they were from the health dept. They told him they had been sent to give him a physical examination, since he was on medicare. One of the men carried what resembled a doctor's bag in his hand. It all seemed legitimate to the old man. They asked Flint to go into the bedroom, remove all of his clothes and call them when he was ready.

When Flint called that he was ready, the men went into the room and one of them played the role of doctor while the other stood by. After they left the old man began to put on his clothes. To his surprise his wallet was missing. He ran out the door but the two men had gone. Flint lost all of his money and the crooks got away. To the best of my knowledge, no one was ever apprehended for this crime.

Ralph Peterson Jr. came to Berkeley County in a meat box. I was told this story by Silas Fields. According to Silas, Ralph Jr. was so mean that the townspeople in a small town in upstate South Carolina, had come up with a plan to kill him.

It seems Ralph had one good friend by the name of Troy, who helped him out of town by making a box with cracks in it, in order for Ralph to breathe on his sojourn via a boxcar on the railroad. Troy marked the box, 'meat' several times on the outside. He put ole Ralph Jr. in the meat box and shipped him by train to Moncks Corner, SC. Troy then drove to Moncks Corner in his pick-up truck and picked up the 'meat' box at the train depot. Ralph settled in a nearby town and lived out his days there, but no doubt his life had been saved by Troy. Ralph Jr. was a tough customer but he settled his rowdy ways after the 'meat' box incident.

This gentleman whom everyone referred to as Dr. Joseph, was a prominent doctor in Berkeley County in the ole days. I remember going into his office several times and he had shelves stocked with gallon jugs of medicine of different colors. When my medicine bottle was empty, I would take it back to be refilled. Before refilling it, Dr. Joseph would always ask me, "What color was the last one I gave you?"

Doctor Joseph would smoke and drink but he spoke out against both. A friend told me the doctor would always tell him to quit smoking but as he was leaving the Dr. would walk with him to the door and ask for a cigarette. Dr. Joseph once asked me if I drank beer. I told him, "Yes, I do." He said, "Don't tease yourself with beer, if you are going to drink, then drink whiskey!"

Sam Winningham was a good man but could get upset real fast. He was in the 'CCC' back in the late thirties. He would always dress in green with a red handkerchief hanging from his back pocket. A ruckus between a couple of 'hotheads' got started near one of the church's and although Sam wasn't involved he sure wanted to be. He began pacing in front of the church, making this statement, "My name is Sam, I don't give a damn. I'll walk through hell with my hat in my hand."

Ash Hadley sold plants of all types in Berkeley County back several years ago. During the winter he also sold turnips and collards. His collards always had worm holes in them and one of his customers asked him what he could do about the holes. Ash's answer was, "Just eat them the same as you would eat a doughnut...eat around the holes."

Robert Dalton said he had the perfect recipe for a fantastic chicken bog. "Get a large iron pot and fill it with water from the Black River. Then take it to your church and have a good old fashioned foot washing in it. After the foot washing, add your chicken, your rice and plenty of salt and pepper. This will make a first class chicken bog every time!"

A gentleman who graduated from Macedonia High School in the late thirties, considered himself a 'woman's man' in his youth. During a re-union of about ten classes a couple of years ago, he was selected to seat the different classes in their respective areas. As he called out the first class to be seated he told them rather sadly, "Come on down here to me and I will give you a hug. That's about all I can do for you now, as age has finally caught up with me."

Bertha Creech was raised in Berkeley County and attended school during my own school days in Macedonia, South Carolina. After leaving school she went to the city of North Charleston and got a job. After working for a week, Bertha came home to visit for the weekend. She was walking around with her friends, Nora and Kelsey, when they passed by some pine trees. Bertha asked her friends, "What kind of trees are those?" Disgustedly Nora told her, "Shut your mouth! You have only been gone to town for a week and you don't even recognize a pine tree!"

Since Raymond Gilbert had retired he loved to go deer hunting. One day he was out scouting the area for a big buck when a doe deer ran right out in front of him. He quickly shot her for he desperately wanted venison steaks for supper. He knew it was illegal but he was willing to take his chances.

In just a few minutes the game warden by the name of Crosley came up to him and asked "Where is that deer you shot?" Caught in the act, Raymond showed the deer to the determined game warden. After he had checked the deer to determine its' gender, Crosley told Raymond that he would have to write him up for killing a doe deer.

Raymond said he pleaded with the game warden to no avail. He finally told the warden, "You have taken my family's supper right off my table." The warden charged him and took the deer. I suspect he had venison for supper that night.

Now this same game warden had a speech impediment and had trouble saying words that started with 's'. He once caught a man and charged him with killing several summer ducks. Ole Crosley took the man before the judge to be prosecuted.

The judge asked Crosley, "What are the charges?" After trying to say 'summer ducks' for several moments the frustrated game warden blurted out, "Your honor, I charge him with killing too many hot weather ducks!"

Frankie Hall told me that he really had it made. He was retired with several checks coming to his mailbox, with all the money he needed to carry him the rest of his life. Then he said "I am a Christian and a member of the church. When I die, I can spend eternity with the Lord in Heaven." I must agree with this man. He truly had it made.

This gentleman said they were looking for a one armed man to pass the collection plate at his church... there is no way a one armed man can hold the collection plate and steal at the same time!

Wade Brock retired and decided he would raise hogs to supplement his income and it would give him something to do. He didn't keep records on his operation so he didn't know how he was doing until one day his son suggested he should keep records. He began keeping entries on his sales and expenses. When taking a load of top hogs to the market a body can pick up a nice big check but unless one knows how expenses are running there is no way to figure out the profit.

Wade began keeping a record of his feed bill and other miscellaneous items. It wasn't too long before he realized he would be far better off *not* raising hogs. He took all of his hogs to the market and that was the end of that!

Monty Fillmore decided he would start a hog operation. He worked on a job but his father, Jake, was retired. Monty told his father, "I will buy the hogs and feed, if you will tend to the hogs. We can then split the profits." He bought fifty young hogs and two thousand bushels of shelled corn. After they had fenced up several acres of land behind his father's house, they set up twelve fifty-five gallon drums of corn with water on it to make it ferment. Sour corn will fatten a hog faster than dry corn.

After several months, these hogs began to top out, and Monty began taking them to the market. He kept careful records and after selling all of them, he decided to go out of business. When asked about his operation Monty said the profit was small and did not warrant his staying in the business, but he reckoned the hog compost on the land was worth something.

Old man Flen Morris was listening to the conversation and remarked, "Buddy, anytime you have to figure hog manure for your profit, you need to start worrying about your money!"

Cotton Farley worked the 12-8 hour shift and had just come in from work on a Saturday morning. Before he could get into the house, a station wagon loaded with women from a church pulled into his drive way. They asked him if he lived there and he said 'yes'. They asked him if that was his house, if the tractor under the shed belonged to him and how about the car and truck in the garage? The answer was 'yes' to all the questions. One of the ladies, said, "You are a young man to have acquired so much worldly goods in your lifetime." Cotton, tired and cranky, answered her, "If you ladies would get off your rear ends, go to work and stop bothering people, I do believe you could own something in your own lifetime!" He then walked into the house and slammed the door. I doubt he was ever bothered with these ladies again!

David Service lived on the outer edge of Berkeley County. He would catch deer dogs when he could and take them home with him. He tied the dogs in his yard and sent word to the owner that he had his dogs. There were no phones then, so he either had to go to the person or send a post card in the mail. When the owners came for his dogs, David would always have a sad story to tell him about how the hunter's dog had killed twelve of his wife's chickens. The owner of the dogs would have to pay David's wife before he could get his dogs.

Word got around among the hunters. You can be sure they tried to get their dogs before they left the area near David's house.

Ole Hoss Jones told me that honey bees can tell when their master or owner dies. They leave the area and will not come back. He said the only way they will stay is if you paint a cross or an x on each hive of bees. I don't have any facts on this so you can be the judge. Actually I suspect once the owner of the bees dies, they might be neglected and find better pickings elsewhere!

Chapter Seventeen

Ike Benner had a good ole mule named Jim. In the summer, he worked this mule all week on the farm. When Saturday came, Ike would load his wagon with produce and vegetables and take them to the market in McCellanville with ole Jim pulling the lot. Sunday morning old Jim had to pull the entire family in the wagon to church, about five miles one way. Sunday night it was back to church again.

Old Jim didn't get much rest and as the years passed he began to slow down. Ike took a piece of barb wire and attached it to the end of his whip. When old Jim got a little too slow, Ike would rap him under the belly with the barb wire whip. The old mule would find another gear. I saw this mule try to kick the front of the wagon to pieces when he was hit with that awful whip. Ole Jim had a rough life in this world and I hope there is a mule heaven somewhere, as he certainly deserves it.

The SPCA would have had their work cut out for them in the old days because a mule had to go when his master called on him. A man farming with a mule did not have time to coax him along. I have seen a man stick a mule in his rear end with a pitch fork. This painful practice would certainly get the ole mule moving fast. A mule had a hard life and when they saw you coming with a bridle in your hand, they knew they would be caught and have to work, so they tried to stay away from you.

Diana Parsons worked with the SPCA. She asked me one day if I knew a man by the name of Creech. I said 'yes' and she told me he had asked her to come to his place to help him de-horn some goats. Diana met with Creech and they began to work with her tools, but it was too slow for him. He said, "I'll be right back." A few minutes later ole Creech was back with his cutting torch and began cutting the horns off the goats. He said "I can do a better job with my ole torch than you can do with your dang tools." They finished the job with the torch. Diana said she had never seen this done before or since and was really undecided what to do with Creech. She said it would be a borderline case for the SPCA.

Mike Fillmore had a date with a young lady in the community by the name of Sadie Simmons. When Mike came to pick Sadie up, her father, Big Bob, came out and sat down in the back seat. Then Sadie came out and sat down on the passenger side of the front seat. Mike looked over at the ole man Simmons and said, "I have a date with your daughter! I didn't ask you to come along!" The ole man said, "If you wait to be *asked*, you don't get to go nowhere." He sat there until his wife, Marcella, came out and joined them. They all went riding together as a foursome.

Damon Scott says that he lives by this theory: "Take no time just getting even, because you can't get ahead by just getting even!"

Harold Hamburg said he was a young boy when his older brother Mickey, got drafted for the army. Times were hard and as his brother started to leave he gave Harold a fifty cent piece with a slap on his rear end. Mickey told young Harold, "I'll see you later, little buddy!" Harold never saw Mickey again as he was a casualty of World War II. Mickey Hamburg is now resting beneath one of those little white crosses on foreign land in a national cemetery with many others from South Carolina.

Packrat Lewis had to walk everywhere he went in the ole days, as he didn't own a car or a mule. He wasn't able to pack a lunch so he kept several ears of corn in his pockets. When he got hungry, he would shell some of the corn off the cob and eat it while walking along the roads. Things have sure changed since those days. We can now get something to eat or a cold drink at a restaurant, store or gas station while traveling the highways.

A man I knew went into business with a friend and they formed a partnership. As time went on they had their ups and downs. They could not agree too well on methods of doing business so they decided to dissolve the partnership. This gentleman told me later that a partnership was the darndest ship he ever tried to sail. I don't think he was married!

Becky Cornett buys new dresses regularly. She puts them in her closet for a while before she wears them. When she decides to wear one and her husband Phil notices, he will always ask, "Honey, is that a new dress?" She answers him honestly, "No, I have had this dress in the closet for a *long* time." Very sneaky, but it does work!

Fred Isom said he grew up in the early part of the century. His parents didn't have much education so when they got a prescription filled at the drug store and it said, 'shake well before taking medicine' on the label, his mother shook him, then made him jump up and down on one foot and then the other for several minutes. She wanted to be sure he was well shaken before she gave him the medicine.

Carl Stevens said he stopped in a restaurant for lunch, with the intention of having fried frog legs if they served them. When the tired, overworked, and somewhat older waitress came over to his table Carl asked her "Mam, do you happen to have frog legs?" She was outraged and told him, "Hell no! I have rheumatism...that's why I walk this way!"

We were raised by the theory that if the shoe fits, wear it and if the truth hurts, just learn to bear it.

Jessie Simpson went down to the sea coast in the ole days and picked up a load of oysters. He tried selling them by going door to door in the community. Times were hard and people wanted the oysters on credit. Jessie took his oysters and dumped them in the woods rather than sell them on credit! I wonder what Jessie would do if he was living today and saw everything being paid by credit card!

Donald Henson drove a school bus in Berkeley County. This particular night he had driven a bus load of students and football players to the school house for a ball game. After the game was over he took everyone safely home and parked the bus. Evidently he didn't notice that he had parked on an incline. When he got out of the bus, it began to roll forward. Donald was walking along and suddenly he was caught between the side of the bus and a tree. He called for help and his family woke and ran to his aid. They took him to the hospital but he had severe internal injuries. The doctors could not save his life. He was a good young man and came from a good family. This was a tragedy and a sad day in Berkeley County.

Greg Scott was a little on the rough side and often spent time in jail. The last time he was arrested, the policeman in charge overlooked the knife Greg always carried in his pocket. As the jailer was making his rounds he found Greg in his cell, his throat cut. He was stone cold! It is always sad when a life is lost in this desperate way.

Aaron Covey was magistrate of a small town in Berkeley County. One day he called his constable, Doug, to go with him to serve a warrant on Jackson Price. They picked Jackson up and Doug started driving toward the jailhouse, with Aaron on the passenger side. Unbeknownst to the lawmen, Jackson, seated on the rear seat, with handcuffs on, pulled a knife. He quickly reached over the front seat and stabbed the magistrate in the chest.

Aaron Covey died at the scene but Doug was able to subdue the prisoner. Jackson Price spent several years in prison and finally went to the electric chair.

Cecil Hall said as a young man in the depression years, he got a job dipping turpentine. The turpentine could only be found in long needle pine trees. Cecil and his co-workers, would take two pieces of flat metal, drive then into a tree with the ends toward the center, pointing downward. Under the two flat pieces of metal would be a metal box on a nail. As the turpentine would 'bleed' from the tree, it would run down these flat pieces of metal causing it to drip down into the metal boxes.

Every so often a man would come by and dump the metal boxes of turpentine into a bucket. When the bucket was full, it would be dumped into a large barrel. A company bought the turpentine and it was taken to a plant to be processed. The men carrying the buckets of turpentine always had their shoes and pants coated with it as it spilled from the buckets on the walk to the barrels. Some of the men remarked that their pants would stand up by themselves when they pulled them off at night. It did help keep the red bugs and ticks off of them as they made their rounds through the bug infested woods.

Chapter Eighteen

My mother gave me instructions on how to make good strong lye soap. Back in the ole days Octagon soap was about all you could buy in the country stores and most people didn't have money to waste on such *nonsense*. A *smart* woman made her own soap for washing clothes, dishes, and younguns, or scrubbing wooden floors, and cleaning any thing else which needed to be cleaned. It would get the job done quickly and efficiently and didn't cost much. I should mention it was used for all necessary bathing and shampooing. Some women swore the strong soap tempered with rain water, was the best beauty treatment possible for one's hair. One thing for sure, I'll bet they never had a problem with lice. A bug couldn't live on a body that used soap made with Red Devil Lye!

It was standard procedure to butcher hogs and cure the meat on the farm in winter weather.

After butchering the hogs, the women folk would skin off the fat, put it in a large iron wash pot in the yard and proceed to heat it until the grease came out. This was called 'rendering' lard. They left the hot grease in the pot as they took out the skin with the dried fat on it. This skin was called cracklings and was used by some people to put in cornbread thereby calling it 'crackling corn bread'. Some people enjoyed eating these cracklings with baked sweet potatoes. This is a true Southern dish.

Next the women would take Red Devil Lye and added it to this hot grease, mixing it well. After boiling this mixture for a while, they allowed it to cool. Then they would slice in into small pieces to be used for house-hold cleaning. It would have to 'cure' for a few days before being used. The women took pride in the color and firmness of their home-made soap.

Clarence Philpot told me that as a boy he helped his mother wash clothes for different families in the community, for fifty cents a load. Some days they were able to wash clothes for two families, thereby earning one dollar.

On wash day, the first thing you had to do was cut wood and build a fire in order to heat the wash pot. Then you had to carry the water from an open well or pump it from a hand pump to fill up the wash pot. I knew some who carried their water from the creek or the river. And then the work began for the clothes had to be scrubbed on the ole wash board with lye soap and they had to be rinsed a couple of times in clean water before they were hung up on a line to dry with wooden clothes-pins. When the clothes were dry they would be taken in and sorted and 'dampened down' to iron. They were then ironed with a cast iron which had been heated on the stove. A person needed several of these irons, in order to have one hot at all times. Some of them had wooden handles which were interchangeable. Others were all cast and one had to use a pot holder or heavy dish clothe to hold them by, in order not to get burned. It was a hard procedure for the woman of the house and I can remember my mama's hands being rough and bleeding from scrubbing all day on the wash board. I can remember other times when she sported nasty burns from ironing. It's no wonder women don't particularly care for the term 'good ole days'.

Cooking was another hard chore. We cooked on a stove fueled by wood. It was great in the cold winter months for us kids to sit beside and take a nap behind, or sometimes even under it when we were small. When I think of it now, it must have been misery for the women-folk...as well as the one who had to do the wood chopping to keep it going day in and day out. In the winter the woman of the house would have to get up early and start a fire in the cold kitchen. Of course there would most likely be a fire in one or two of the other rooms, but the heat never extended to the kitchen where the buckets of drinking water we had hauled in the night before would be frozen over with ice.

A body could stand in front of the fireplace and the back side of us would still nearly freeze solid, it seemed. Our faces would be burning and our butts cold or just the opposite. There seemed to be no happy medium. But the truth was we knew no better so we took it all in stride.

When I was a child, I guess, like all children, I took it for granted when my mother always built the fire and had the kitchen good and warm for us children, with the smell of breakfast cooking, when we got out of bed. The work was hard but there was something special about the old wood stove and mama cooking breakfast on a cold winter morning, which can never be replaced.

In the summer it was just the opposite. Mom would have to stand over the cook stove in the hot South Carolina weather, canning enough vegetables to feed us children for the winter, while still preparing our meals. The sweat would pour down her face, but she worked on, never complaining, never missing a lick, when it came to what she felt was her 'job'.

The house would be so hot that after supper we would all gather on the porch, looking for a cool breeze. The nights would probably be miserably hot, but somehow we seldom noticed. And through heat and cold, we survived without the benefit of air conditioners or heat pumps.

I remember how as children we always looked forward to playing outside every chance we got. We had a lot of chores to do and with going to school and helping out at home, there wasn't a whole lot of time for play. We enjoyed it to the fullest when we did have the time to romp and run with our friends or cousins. We never really noticed when the weather was too hot or too cold. I have to smile when I hear children today complaining about going outside and leaving the air conditioning in the summer or the heat in winter. But I feel sad when I think of all the naive fun the kids of today miss out on when they are glued to the television or the computer or all the numerous video games available. Personally I don't envy them a bit.

I often think today of how the women in our families never wasted anything. They were re-cycling before the word was ever invented. I have quilts made by my grandmother which has tiny slivers of material worked into it, stitched carefully by hand to last forever, it seems. I remember the quiet moments of watching her as she worked, talking all the while, never missing a tiny, delicate stitch.

Chapter Nineteen

Ike Bently was talking with his neighbor George Albin. Ike told ole George there were two things he wanted to get rid of but hadn't been able to do so. He said one was the Jerusalem weed and the other was the Methodist people. George told him, "I don't know how to get rid of the Methodist people but if you pour some whiskey on those weeds, the Baptist people will dig them up to get the alcohol!" Of course I really don't know how true that is.

A church was having a baptismal service on a Sunday afternoon. There were several young ladies sitting on the front bench waiting to be baptized. As one of the young ladies, lovely Doris Wilson, got up to be baptized, her robe fell off. Pastor Dennis said, "Don't look on her nakedness as you might go blind." Old Dixie Patton, sitting up front, covered one eye with his hand and remarked, "I'm willing to risk the sight in one eye!"

Flossie Johnson told about growing old in this fashion: "I don't remember growing old but somehow I guess I did. It seems like only yesterday that I was just a kid. I remember following daddy through the fields of fresh plowed dirt and running to mama to kiss away a hurt. We picked wild flowers and black berries that grew along the lane and we enjoyed the shade of the big oak tree and running barefoot in the rain. We wore faded shirts and dungarees with patches on the knees but we had happiness and love."

"Time passed and soon my life was filled with a teenager's dreams and graduation, friends, dates, proms and things to come. So life went on like an endless chain that changed from day to day, then I found that old age had appeared and youth had slipped away."

Now just as clouds have silver linings and rainbows their pot of gold, I have a million memories but I don't remember growing old."

A church in the neighborhood had just closed out a good revival. Several people were saved and asked to join the church. The preacher was very excited as he called them up front. "Look at all these *convicts!*" He shouted. I think he meant to say '*converts*'.

One gentleman said that when the preacher came to visit he met him on the porch with this remark: "Run, chickens, run, here comes the preacher!" Preacher James used to say, "You just let them chickens live! I would rather have me a good pot of collard greens anytime!" He was a rarity.

Ash Wentworth said he was sitting on his porch when the preacher came to visit him. As they were sitting there talking, a little chicken came out from under the porch. In all seriousness Ash told the little chicken, "You had better get back under that porch. The fellow sitting here with me has already eaten your mama and your daddy and he's just a waiting for you to grow up!"

Dale Cootze said he thought he had been called to preach so he discussed it with his pastor. As they were talking about it the pastor asked him why he thought he had been called to preach. Dale's answer was, "I *love* fried chicken!"

Gimp Porter said he had been preaching some around the country and decided to get his license. His co-worker, Bill, and he didn't get along too well but they tried to keep out of each others way. When Bill found out Gimp had become a licensed minister, he went to see him and said, "Now that you have become a minister, you can't show any malice toward me." The newly made minister said, "I didn't like you before I became a minister and I certainly don't like you now!"

Elton Cox was a rural mail carrier during the depression. Letters could be mailed with a three cent stamp. As he was making his rounds one day, a man was waiting at his mail box with a letter in his hand to be mailed. He said to Elton, "This letter has to be mailed today but I don't have the money for a stamp!" Elton took his letter with him and bought the stamp out of his own pocket. It was difficult during the depression years in terms of money, but I suspect the examples of human kindness often shown by one's neighbor might have made up for a lot of the hardships.

Galen Hall was up in age and had to use a hearing aid in one ear. This particular day he went to the doctor with a miner ailment and the doctor gave him a suppository to take home with him. Later in the day he realized he wasn't hearing real well, so he removed the hearing aid which turned out to be the suppository. After checking the suppository he smiled and said, "Now I know where my hearing aid is!" I have to say I really don't know how true this little story is!

Ole Martin Gross turned sixty-five and retired from his job. Having nothing else to do, he began hanging out at the local bar. One day Vera Prince came in for a couple of drinks and made conversation with him. She asked him, "What do you do for a living?" Martin's answer was, "I chase women." Vera then asked him, "What do you do when you catch them?" His answer was, "Nothing!"

A lady stood up in church one Sunday and said, "You all please pray for me! I need your prayers and Lord knows you people need the practice!" I wasn't there that particular Sunday but I heard it was the gospel truth!

This gentleman was an engineer on the railroad and his run took him over the mountains and through the valleys. He said life reminded him of a mountain railroad and to make this run successful, you must make it from the cradle to the grave. I felt this was good, common sense.

During the depression years life was difficult for practically everyone. Things began to get better here in our little Southern county when the International Paper Mill started up in Georgetown and Westvaco started up their first machine in 1937. They started up the #2 machine in 1947 and the #3 machine in 1957.

The two paper mills in Berkeley County gave several thousand people, jobs on three shifts each day, plus the woodland divisions, who were the ones who sawed and hauled pulp wood. In recent years they added a chip service.

When the Japanese bombed Pearl Harbor on December 7th, 1941, provoking the USA to get involved in World War II, the Navy Yard in Charleston, SC, began serious work. It was then of course that young men began receiving their 'greetings' or draft notices from Uncle Sam. Older men and lots of women began working at the Naval Bases, Air Force Bases and Army Bases. I guess we can say this was the end of the great depression.

Around 1938 this old bootlegger told some of his friends, "My moonshine business is doing good, but you men need jobs so I am going to help you out." He told them to get some carpenter tools ready as "We are going to need a new school house." In a few days the old Macedonia School burned to the ground. The investigation never resulted in finding anyone responsible for the fire.

Those of us who were going to Macedonia at the time can remember the string of small low buildings that were put up fast to accommodate the pupils. We referred to these buildings as 'goat sheds'. They served their purpose until the new school house was completed. The class of 1940 graduated from this new building.

On January 9th, 1941, the first young men from Berkeley County reported to the draft board in Moncks Corner to be transported to Fort Jackson for training, in what later became World War II. Very few of these men are living today.

Mack Willis was very good at raising cows and keeping his feed bill at a low rate at the same time. In the spring of the year, some people would burn large areas of forest and in a few days the green grass would start growing. Cows loved to graze on the tender grass and would begin to put on weight. Mack let his cows run loose in the woods, graze on this grass, eat tender young leaves, moss off of trees, and wild herbs.

This would take care of his cattle until winter time came. Then Mack had another trick to obtain free food for his cattle. I was told by some of the large landowners that ole Mack would put a couple of cows in the back of his truck and take them to one of the plantations at night. He would back his truck up to the fence until the cows could jump over. He would then get the fence back in shape the best way he could and head for home.

Mack kept track of where his cattle were 'boarded' and he would leave them there all winter if the landowners didn't spot them. In most cases, having cows of their own, they probably wouldn't notice a couple of stray cows. If they did find a stray cow they would put the word out to their neighbors. When Mack heard about it he would always go to the plantation owners and tell them he had lost a cow and would like to look at their stray cattle. Of course since it was his cow he would take her home.

Ole Mack was as crooked as they come, but you have to give it to him; he had a lot of ingenuity when it came to the style of his crooked ways. If some of them old Berkeley County boys spent as much time working on something worth-while as they did working up to doing something illegal, it's un-telling what they might have accomplished.

The Henry Dupree house in the Macedonia Community, built in the 1800's He raised his family here and lived to be 100 years old.

Stephen Guerry Home located in the Macedonia Community, built in 1800's

UNITED STATES OF AMERICA
OFFICE OF PRICE ADMINISTRATION

WAR RATION BOOK TWO

IDENTIFICATION

319766 EC

Jettie Cordell Shuler
(Name of person to whom book is issued)

Shulerville *S.C.* *16* *M*
(City or post office) (State) (Age) (Sex)

ISSUED BY LOCAL BOARD No. *46-8-1* *Berkeley* *S.C.*
(County) (State)

319766EC
Moncks Corner
(City)

(Street address of local board)

By *Mrytrie B. Bishop*
(Signature of issuing officer)

SIGNATURE
(To be signed by the person to whom this book is issued. If such person is unable to sign because of age or incapacity, another may sign in his behalf)

WARNING

1 This book is the property of the United States Government. It is unlawful to sell or give it to any other person or to use it or permit anyone else to use it, except to obtain rationed goods for the person to whom it was issued.

2 This book must be returned to the War Price and Rationing Board which issued it, if the person to whom it was issued is inducted into the armed services of the United States, or leaves the country for more than 30 days, or dies. The address of the Board appears above.

3 A person who finds a lost War Ration Book must return it to the War Price and Rationing Board which issued it.

4 PERSONS WHO VIOLATE RATIONING REGULATIONS ARE SUBJECT TO $10,000 FINE OR IMPRISONMENT, OR BOTH.

OPA Form No. R-121

World War II ration book – They were issued to all civilians during the War.

INSTRUCTIONS

1 This book is valuable. Do not lose it.

2 Each stamp authorizes you to purchase rationed goods in the quantities and at the times designated by the Office of Price Administration. Without the stamps you will be unable to purchase those goods.

3 Detailed instructions concerning the use of the book and the stamps will be issued from time to time. Watch for those instructions so that you will know how to use your book and stamps.

4 Do not tear out stamps except at the time of purchase and in the presence of the storekeeper, his employee, or a person authorized by him to make delivery.

5 Do not throw this book away when all of the stamps have been used, or when the time for their use has expired. You may be required to present this book when you apply for subsequent books.

Rationing is a vital part of your country's war effort. This book is your Government's guarantee of your fair share of goods made scarce by war, to which the stamps contained herein will be assigned as the need arises.

Any attempt to violate the rules is an effort to deny someone his share and will create hardship and discontent.

Such action, like treason, helps the enemy.

Give your whole support to rationing and thereby conserve our vital goods. Be guided by the rule:

"*If you don't need it,* **DON'T BUY IT.**"

☆ U. S. GOVERNMENT PRINTING OFFICE 1942 16—30559-1

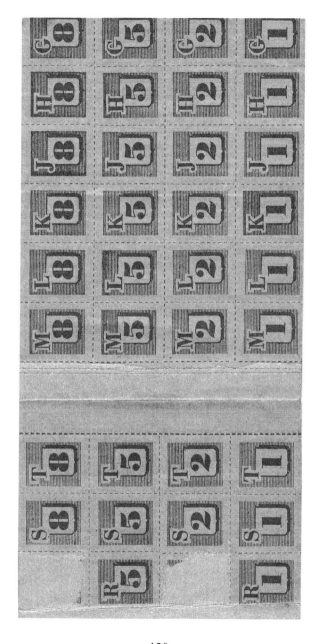

Dennis Shuler after the War ended in Europe in 1945. Picture taken in a town in the Po Valley somewhere in Northern Italy.

Dennis Shuler during basic training at Fort McClellan, Alabama in 1943.

Dennis Shuler with his mule Alice.

House built by Blease and Virginia Dupree in 1947.

**Dennis Shuler and Gamewell Brown taken at the museum in
Moncks Corner, S.C.**

**Dennis Shuler with a mounted black bear at the Dennis
Wildlife Center in Bonneau.**

124

Dennis Shuler's friend Gamewell Brown at the Hellhole Festival in Jamestown, S.C. Taken by a moonshine liquor distiller.

Lewis Hardee with a horse-drawn buggy – transportation in the "old days."

Sleeping quarters at Fort Jackson, S.C. during World War I in 1917. Dennis Shuler's Dad, Elvin, trained here and was a Corporal during this war.

Old Navy Yard bus that took workers to yard during World War II. Driven by Frank Crawford.

126

Game Jackson house, built in the early 1900's.

Friend Wyndham house located in Macedonia Community. He, his son Calhoun, and now his grandson, Billy, raised their families here.

Log cabin house built by Marion and Mary Thornley in the 1930's with their two oldest boys.

Grammar school building at Macedonia in the old days.

Paul Jackson and Will Judy standing beside their old Chevrolet car.

Chapter Twenty

Cheer up! Even though inflation is real bad, a dime can still be used as a screwdriver.

Old Bill Whitehead used to say, "I can only please one person per day. This is not your day and tomorrow is not looking too good either."

A gentleman I once knew by the name of Rock Helton was living a life of ease, but his family was suffering because he didn't like to work. He just plain refused to do an honest days' work. His little children didn't have shoes to go on their feet and I feel sure they went to bed hungry many times. One of his neighbors decided he would get ole Rock to moving. He sent him a post card through the mail, telling him to get a job and go to work by the following Monday morning or 'We are coming to get you!' He signed the card 'The KKK'. This really got ole Rock motivated and he wasted no time finding a job. This was done without malice to Rock simply to put a fire under his butt, and get him to work for a living. It got the job done.

Of course if such a thing happened today, Rock would probably go to the FBI and the person who sent the 'threatening card' in the mail would be sent to prison, the lazy gent would wind up being on the Jerry Springer Show and would probably sell his story to be made into a movie! Life is strange sometimes!

A small town in Berkeley County had two barber shops during the depression, Manus' and Pete's. Haircuts were twenty-five cents each. Pete wanted to raise prices to thirty-five cents, but Manus would not agree. Ole Pete decided on a strategy. He hired two men to go to the home of his rival, Manus, at night, call him out to their car and let him know what he could expect if he didn't raise his prices.

The reluctant barber agreed to raise his price but he developed a strategy of his own. When a customer paid him thirty-five cents for a haircut, Manus would give them a nickel back. This was a good business practice and it still afforded him the most customers.

Old Paul Orick sat on the front bench in church and often he would go to sleep and snore loud enough to disrupt the preacher. One Sunday morning as he started snoring the preacher called on the man next to him to wake him up. The man shook Paul and said 'The preacher said to wake up!' Paul replied loudly, 'You tell the preacher to make his sermon a little livelier and I will!'

Luke Garrison lived in a cabin near the swamp. One day as I was visiting him, he told me there was a rattlesnake living in his wall. I asked him if he wasn't afraid the snake would come out and bite him. He said, "No, I don't bother him and he doesn't bother me. He's better than a cat when it comes to catching mice and rats and when I want him to sing his rattles, I just knock on the wall. Otherwise I leave him alone and we have a working relationship!" Sounded pretty smart to me.

I knew this gentleman well. He was one of the best marksman in the county. He traded a double barrel Lee Co. Smith to a revenue agent for a five shot Winchester semi-automatic shotgun.

One Saturday morning he went deer hunting with some men in the Blue Springs area of Berkeley County. The dogs jumped and headed toward his stand. He shot once and the dogs quit barking. The other men went to him and he had three deer laid out. He said he only saw one deer running in the bushes when he shot it. He didn't tell this story too often as people didn't believe it, even though he had men with him who could vouch for his story. I have known several people who have killed two deer with one shot. I killed a five point and a nine point with one shot in 1988.

Another time this same gentleman went with two friends up on the Tiger Corner Road. They walked there from home. The driver put the dogs in and he saw five deer almost immediately. He fired into them with his single barrel gun and killed one deer. The other four ran out to this gentleman and he killed all four of them with the Winchester automatic.

They had five deer to carry home on foot. Since they were about three miles away, this gentleman had to walk home, get his mule and wagon, and go back and load the deer and bring them home. I know this to be a fact as the gentleman was my father and I was a teenager at the time.

Jack Henderson used to say it was a gross misreckoning to say a dog was man's best friend. He said he firmly believed it was the house fly. He said when a man was being buried there was usually at least one fly that would be in the casket and he would stay there until the end, making that long, last journey right along with a body!

Berkeley County got its' first funeral home in 1949. A young man established the business in Monck's Corner and ran it for many years. Before this people used funeral homes from other counties or buried the dead themselves.

Back when I was growing up, there were usually people in each community who would come to the aid of a family who lost a loved one. They would bathe the body of the deceased person and put on some of their best clothes to carry them through their journey 'home'. They would then lay the body on what they called 'cooling' boards or a flat structure resembling a table. The deceased would be left in the house in this manner until their friends could get lumber and nails to build a box or coffin. The coffin would be lined with material or sometimes a favorite quilt. The body was then placed in the wooden coffin until the time of the funeral. From the moment of death until the funeral, friends and relatives would gather at the home of the deceased to comfort the family or help them any way they could. The time of the funeral would depend on the weather, as a person not embalmed could not be kept very long without a problem. Men from the community would dig a grave by hand with shovels, in the local cemetery. When the time for the funeral arrived, the men would nail the lid on the coffin, put it in the back of a wagon pulled by a mule or a horse and take it to the church where the funeral would be 'preached'. Later, at the cemetery, the pall bearers would take the coffin from the wagon and place it in the grave. A minister or friend would say a few words and then the family would leave and go back to their home. There the women of the church would have a meal prepared for all who attended the funeral and wanted to participate. After family and friends had left, local men would use hand shovels to fill in the grave and make the mound over it. Thing have certainly changed since then.

This Berkeley County boy we affectionately nicknamed 'Tiger', was in the army during World War II, on the front lines in France. One day ole Tiger looked behind him and there was a German soldier, his rifle at his shoulder and aimed, looking right at him, ready to shoot. Tiger immediately turned around and drew a bead on the German soldier. They both stood there looking at each other with their rifles aimed. Neither could pull the trigger. Tiger said the German soldier took his rifle down, turned his back and slowly walked away. Tiger did the same. As they walked away, ole Tiger and the German soldier looked back over their shoulders at each other. They parted company without firing a shot.

Chapter Twenty-One

A man I knew, by the name of Perry, raised Arabian horses. He said the Arabian horses were trained to cross the desert without drinking much water. In fact they were trained to eat before drinking, even though they might be extremely thirsty. According to Perry, you could set a bucket of feed and a bucket of water before them and if properly trained, the beautiful Arabian horses would eat first. Perry said he taught one, by the name of ole Josh, to count. When he asked Josh the sum of one and one he would stomp his front foot on the ground twice. If Perry asked him the sum of two and two Josh would stomp his foot on the ground four times and so on. When finally Perry asked Josh how many hypocrites were in the church the ole horse would start stomping with all four feet, until he had to be stopped!

Preacher Hiram Dixon said that as a young man he was pastor of a church in Moncks Corner. During revival services a pretty young girl by the name of Betty, would come to his church with a big ole ugly boyfriend. Preacher Hiram said he prayed every night that she would get rid of her ugly boy friend so he could ask her for a date. In just a few nights, his prayers were answered. The young lady came to church by herself and the preacher asked her for a date. Betty accepted and after a short period of courtship she and Hiram were married. The preacher got the pretty girl for his wife and the ole ugly fellow had to go shopping to find him another! But you know the old saying, 'beauty is in the eyes of the beholder.' Ole preacher Hiram's wife might have looked like a dog and he thought she was beautiful!

James Cosco had protruding front teeth. After World War II he got out of the army and went to work at the Ordinance Depot. His friends set him up with a blind date with lovely Pamela. He didn't know it but the girl had agreed to play a joke on him. James was given the name, address and the time to pick Pamela up. He was on time and when he knocked on the door, the young lady met him. After he introduced himself Pamela asked him, "Are you the man that can eat corn off the cob through a picket fence?" Personally, I felt that was a terrible thing for her to say but I have to say ole James got the last laugh...he ended up marrying Pamela and all of their children have teeth just like their daddy's.

A lady I once knew was discussing with the undertaker who had buried her husband, about a headstone to put on his grave. The undertaker asked her what she would like for him to put on his headstone. She said, "After the life he lived here on this earth, I would suggest you put these words, 'Moved to a Warmer Climate'.

Dick Dickson served time on the chain gang. He said it was almost unbearable. He wrote his mother and asked her to bake a cake with a knife in it. He wanted to cut his own throat to get out of the situation. He said the guards were terrible. When they were working on the roads, the guards kept trying to get him to go across the ditch to pick up a can or piece of paper. He said, "I knew they would shoot me and then claim I was trying to run away." He also told me that he saw another Berkeley County man take a guard's head off with a grubbing hoe while they were on the chain gang together in Florida.

Lige Hall loved to square dance and often held dances in his home, back in the old days. The dances were usually held on a Saturday night, for after drinking a lot of moonshine whiskey, ole Lige, his boys, and all their friends, knew they could recuperate on Sunday. One particular Saturday night, Lige hired a young man by the name of Smith, to play music for the dance. After playing constantly into the wee hours of the morning, Smith decided to call it a night. Lige asked him to play on as he had just gotten in the mood to dance. Smith said rather vehemently, "No, I am going to go on home! It's past one in the morning!" The old gentleman called two of his boys together and said, "Take Smith out in the yard and see if you can convince him to play music a while longer." The three of them went out in the yard and a few minutes later they came back into the house. Blood was coming out of the Smith's nose and head. He picked up his guitar and played with vigor until they allowed him to go home. I feel sure, without a doubt, Smith never accepted another invitation to play music at Lige's house.

In the early forties, Nathan Rivers, along with his mother, Kate, came from another state to make their home in the lower part of Berkeley County. They both found jobs and after a period of time, Nathan started working for Floyd Mitchell, who ran a small restaurant. Floyd drank a lot and would get drunk for several days at a time. He depended on Floyd to run his business for him and the young man did a remarkable job. As the years passed, Nathan's mother died and eventually he married and had a family. The business did good and Floyd offered to give Nathan part interest in it. It was an oral agreement since they never bothered with legal papers. Nathan devoted all his time and energy to running the restaurant. Out of the blue, Floyd got an offer for the business and sold it. Selfishly he kept all of the money and Nathan was left with no job and no means to provide for his family. He tried several jobs but was never satisfied with any of them. He became depressed over the situation and one Sunday morning, he was found lying across his mother's grave in a cemetery in Berkeley County. He had a pistol wound to his head. This was a tragedy as he not only lost his life but he also left behind a beautiful family and many friends who loved him. Although many years have passed, I still treasure his friendship and memories.

Bubba Helton was inducted into the army in 1942. His grandmother passed away in 1943. After being notified by his family, Bubba went to his commanding officer and asked for leave to attend the funeral. His commanding officer questioned him, "How close were you and your grandmother?" Bubba replied, "About twenty miles."

Back during the depression, there were a lot of squirrels and rabbits put on the table. This probably kept many people from starving. A certain time of the year 'wolves' would bore under the skin of a rabbit or squirrel and cause the skin to bulge out, thus resulting in the afflicted animal being thrown away. One day Howard Simpleton told his father he had killed a rabbit but had to throw it away since it had two 'wolves' in it. His father asked him where the 'wolves' were located. Young Simpleton's answer was "Between his hind legs!" His father was a bit upset at losing the game, since he knew all male rabbits were endowed with the same thing. But the scary part is that Howard was turned loose with a gun! Perhaps I should explain at this point that 'wolves' were tiny boring creatures that feasted on other animals, thus eventually resulting in the animal's death. I don't know the proper name for them, only that the old folks called them 'wolves'.

This gentleman was retired and he loved to raise a garden and he often sold vegetables, after his family had used all they needed and he had given the neighbors all they wanted. One day a man came to visit him and made this remark "When I was a child, I loved to play in the dirt but I'm grown now and you won't catch me messing around in the dirt anymore!" Personally, I think many of us would benefit by a little 'messing around in the dirt.'

A few days before mother's day, two good friends, Ben and Bill were talking. Bill asked Ben, "What are you going to give your wife for mother's day?" Ben's answer was, "Nothing. She hasn't used what I gave her last Mother's

137

day." Bill asked "What did you give her?" Ben's answer was: "A cemetery plot". Talk about cheap, wishful thinking!

Grant Folly owned a large herd of cattle. One day he was riding his horse along the road near his house. Some of his dogs were running along beside him. A salesman came by and ran over one of the dogs. The salesman stopped and tried to apologize but Grant had a vicious temper. With a cow whip in his hand, he chopped off part of the salesman's ear without giving it a second thought.

Hickory Smith's sister was married to Grant. One Sunday afternoon, Hickory, who had always been close to his sister, decided to surprise her and her family, with a visit. As he walked up on the porch, he heard Grant cursing and abusing his sister. Hickory jumped off the porch and found him a good stick. He ran back onto the porch, threw the door open and fell on his brother-in-law with that big stick. He beat Grant so badly he had to spend a couple of days in the hospital. After he came home from the hospital, Hickory approached him with this remark, "When you get well, don't take it out on my sister! I still have my stick and I have plenty more to give you!" Although I'm not sure his kind of stick is the answer, I do feel families don't 'stick' together anymore. If that happened today, quite likely the brother would say it was none of his business and leave.

The residents on Highway six, right outside of Moncks Corner, were losing cows out of their barns and could not locate any cow tracks leaving their yards. The long arm of the law finally caught up with the crooks! Those suckers were putting lace-up rubber boots on the cows before they led them out of the yard. This neat trick worked for quite a while.

Ole Stingy Grand's brother, Stash, lived in another state when he passed on to the other side. Ole Stingy checked with a funeral home about the cost of sending a hearse to get Stash. The price was higher than Ole Stingy felt was necessary so he rented a trailer, hooked it behind his car and went to bring Stash home. He strapped the casket onto the trailer and returned to Berkeley County, where ole Stash was buried in peace.

Harry and James were hunting together one day when they saw the game-warden, Horace Fields, approaching them. Harry had a hunting license, but James didn't have one. Harry told James, "You stand still and I will run so ole Horace will think I don't have a license!" He took off as fast as he could run with the game warden in hot pursuit. After running a ways, Harry sat down on a log and waited for the game warden to catch up with him. When ole Horace caught up with Harry, huffing and puffing, he demanded, "Let me see your license!"

Harry pulled out his license and handed it to Horace. The warden then said to him, "Since you have a license why on earth did you run?" Harry's answer was, "I got me a license so I ran to lead you away from my buddy. He don't have one." Harry was too honest for his own good.

Abe Fairbanks and his wife, Callie went to visit some friends they hadn't seen in quite a while. They were received warmly and were seated on the couch while their friends prepared supper for them. Abe later reported to anyone who would listen, "I smelled a peculiar odor and began looking around to find it. I looked behind the couch we were sitting on and saw a little dog looking back at me. I finally figured it out! The little dog had evidently eat a belly full of lima beans and was doing his 'thing'. I told my wife, 'let's go!' I don't even want to drink water where there's a dog in the house. In my opinion a man can lower himself to the status of a dog but a dog cannot elevate himself to the status of a man." Personally I am sure women are glad now that most people call on the phone before they visit. This gives them time to put the dog out and straighten the house a bit.

Mike Tabor came to Berkeley County from up north, at the age of nineteen, to seek his fortune. He loved animals and decided Santee Swamp would be a good place for him to settle down. He got permission from a man on the river road to pitch a tent. He made friends with the local people and bought all types of wild animals from them. At one time in 1932, he had forty alligators in one pen.

Mike's business was doing good but he began to find the nights lonely by himself. He managed to buy a radio from Sears and Roebuck, which helped some, but he still needed a companion. At the age of twenty-six, he met and married a young black girl. South Carolina did not perform mixed marriages at the time, therefore they had to get a friend to drive them to Washington, D.C. to be married.

Eleven children were born to this couple. The husband delivered seven of the children himself and educated all of them. I met this man after world War II ended and he was a healthy, robust, cheerful man. He came into town on a regular basis, going to the post office or train depot. He was a gentle man but could be tough when the situation warranted it. He passed away a the age of seventy-two and is buried in his yard near the Santee Swamp he loved so well.

A good creed to live by is: "I shall pass through this world but once, any good therefore I can do or any kindness I can show to any human being, let me do it now. Do not let me defer or neglect it for I shall not pass this way again." Some of us here in Berkeley County actually do use the creed from time to time.

Gabe Doolittle said during the depression years, he only had one shirt and one pair of pants. When he came in from work, he had to go to bed while his wife washed his clothes so he could have clean clothes to wear to work the next day.

I was told by an elderly man that back in the ole days these two men by the name of Jake and Henry went squirrel hunting together. They both shot at a squirrel but got into an argument over who had actually killed it. They had a shootout and Jake was killed. I would hate to live my life with the knowledge I had killed another man over a *squirrel.*

Cecil Cowels went to the Buick dealership in Charleston to buy a car. He told the salesman that he owned a Chevrolet but would like to step up to a Buick. "I'm a poor boy and don't have much money," Cecil told the salesman, thinking it would help him get a better deal. To his surprise the salesman said, "If you are a poor boy, you don't have any business on my car lot. I don't have time for you and I'm asking you to leave!"

Slim Strunk was squirrel hunting in Berkeley County, one fine day. He was standing still, looking over some trees, trying to locate a squirrel. He saw a movement on the side of a tree, took aim and fired a shot with his shotgun. To Slim's surprise, he heard a man holler for help. Slim had filled the man, Brian Thornton's, face with small shot. Brian had been standing by a tree in the bushes with his hand resting on the side of the tree. For some reason he moved his hand and Slim took it to be a squirrel. Slim rushed Brian to the hospital where the doctor removed shot from his face and body. The sheriff came to investigate the shooting and after questioning both parties, decided it was an accident. No charges were filed. Slim and Brian knew each other and it was just a freak accident.

I have been told there is a town in Berkeley County that doesn't have a grocery store or a gas station. There are only eleven customers who receive a morning newspaper and they have to go to centrally located mailboxes to pick up their copies. This town was named by a man who came from Alabama to South Carolina many years ago. He purchased a fifty acre tract of land for a summer home and paid for it with a barrel of strained honey.

Allen, Roscoe and Salt went fishing one night in the early fifties on Lake Moultrie, near the power house. A storm came up and the men decided to try to make it to Adkins Landing to find shelter. They had a large boat and

141

motor but the water got terribly rough and flipped the boat upside down. After hanging onto the boat for a while, they decided to let the motor loose from the boat and it quickly sank into the lake. This allowed the boat to rise up a little higher in the water. The scared men realized they were in deep trouble so Roscoe, who was an excellent swimmer, decided he would try to make it to the landing. He made it, but was so exhausted when he finally reached the landing, that he simply fell face down, unable to go any farther. Some men were camped out at the landing waiting for the water to calm down so they could go fishing. One of them saw Roscoe as he came out of the water and fell down. They went to his aid and he told them there were two other men hanging to a capsized boat in the lake. As the water calmed down, the men began searching for the overturned boat. Thankfully they found the men still alive. Salt was lying across the bottom of the overturned boat. The edge of the boat had rubbed the flesh from his stomach. They were sure they were going to a watery grave and were eternally thankful when the boat came to rescue them. Allen was so grateful to the Lord for sending the rescuers that he later became a Baptist minister.

Will McCall had a wife who liked to go shopping with her friends and stay until the stores closed at night before she finally went home. One night as she came in well after dark, Will made this remark, "Even the birds have sense enough to go to roost when dark comes! I'm expecting you to change your shopping habits! From this day on I expect you to be home with the family before dark!" I never did hear if Ole Will's wife obeyed his orders, but personally I doubt it!

Chapter Twenty-Two

Thoughtful but not throughly tested, thoughts: If you ever see an all black baseball team playing a game of baseball against an all white baseball team on a Catholic ball diamond for the benefit of the Jewish people, this will surely be brotherly love.

A senior citizen reported: "I like my bifocals, my dentures fit me fine, my hearing aid is perfect but Lord! How I miss my mind!"

President Reagan wrote this as a tribute to his wife concerning his Rancho Del Cirlo, (Ranch in the Sky) The ranch is on top of a mountain overlooking the Pacific Ocean. "We relax at this ranch, which, if not Heaven itself, surely has the same zip code!"

Preacher Hanes' favorite saying: "Many who wait until the eleventh hour to be saved, often die at ten thirty!"

A friend of mine used to say: "The difference between a working man and a loafing one is only a nickel; and the loafing man has the nickel!"

It is my belief that the worst day fishing is better than the best day working!

One old spinster told me, "women who seek to be equal to men lack ambition!"

Overheard in the feed store one day: "I don't lie, cheat, or steal unnecessarily!"

Seen on a bumper sticker: "Beautify South Carolina, put a Yankee on the bus."

Sign in a nursing home: "Youth is a gift of nature, age is a work of art."

My grandpa used to say: "One indication of middle age is the sudden attraction to naps."

An old preacher I knew liked to say: "No gift is ours until we have thanked the giver."

Al Hendricks was complaining about his bad luck to his neighbor, Jody Williams. Al's wife had run off with his best friend and he was terribly depressed. Jody told him, "Cheer up, you don't have a problem! Just remember: pharaoh lost his whole army in the red sea." What a thing to think of at a time like that!

It *is* a proven fact: people who have the most birthdays, live the longest.

A man I knew by the name of Clem was a very scary person. He lived on a farm with his wife and one night the chickens began making a lot of noise. There had to be a man or a varmint in the chicken house! Clem's wife Annie told him to go see what was bothering the chickens. Clem told her, "I'm not going out there! We can get more chickens but you can't get another husband!"

Sol had a pregnant wife. It was winter and the weather was real cold. As was expected on this cold night his wife woke him up and said, "Honey, you have got to get up and take me to the hospital! I am ready to deliver this baby!" Sol rolled over and made this remark, "Just cross your legs and hold on! I don't plan to get up before daylight!"

Ole Mark was a shrewd business man. One day one of his friends came by his business with a one thousand dollar bill in his hand. He told Mark, "I can get you all of these you want for eight hundred dollars each!" Mark told him, "Let me hold that thousand dollar bill for a little while! I want to be sure it's okay." He took the bill up the street and had it checked by other merchants and they all said it was real money. He got thirty two hundred dollars together which was enough to buy four, one thousand dollar bills. This was enough profit to buy a new car back in the old days.

Mark was ready to make the transaction but his friend said, "We have got to meet this man in Moncks Corner since he has the money." They got together and went to town, renting adjacent rooms at the hotel. It wasn't long

144

before a robber came to Mark's door and robbed him of all his money. After the robber left, Ole Mark went to this friend's room to tell him what had happened. To his surprise, his friend had left town and could not be found.

Ole Art Bellows had finished dinner and decided to buy a popsicle for dessert. As he stood there sucking on his popsicle, he noticed a young man staring at him. Art asked the young man if perhaps he had not seen a man suck a popsicle before. The young man answered, "I have seen men suck popsicles before but I have *never* seen a set of lips like yours wrapped around one!"

Chapter Twenty-Three

Butchering and Home Curing Hogs: back in the old days, people living in the country tried to keep a mule or horse to plow their fields, a good milk cow to get fresh milk, a couple of good brood sows to raise their own meat, and have a few laying hens to get fresh eggs and raise young chickens for the table. They also needed a wagon to be pulled by the mules for transportation, to haul their crops from the fields and haul firewood from the forests.

Most everyone in Berkeley county had some hogs penned up to be butchered when the weather got real cold. These hogs were fed all the dry corn they could eat until they were fat. A corn fed hog had firm meat and a good flavor when butchered.

A day was set aside to butcher hogs and all of us, big and small, got up before daylight to do our share of the work. We dug a hole in the ground, put a fifty five gallon drum in this hole at an angle so that it would hold enough hot water to scald a hog. This water had to be heated just right as water too hot would cause the hair to set up and made it difficult to pull. While the water was being heated, we killed the hogs and brought them to the work area and began the process. We would put the first dead hog's head in the hot water and after waiting for a couple of minutes, a portion of the hog was pulled out of the barrel far enough to pull some hair. If the hair didn't pull good, the hog was put back into the barrel of hot water a little longer. When the hair began to pull sufficiently, the hog was pulled from the barrel of hot water and the other end was put in the barrel. When the hair on this end began to pull well, the hog was removed and put on some boards or pine straw so the cleaning crew could get all the hair off the hog. Another hog was then put in the scalding barrel and this continued until all the hogs were cleaned.

The hogs were then hung up by their hind legs, scraped down and washed clean. They were then ready to be opened up and their intestines and other organs removed. They were washed out with clean water and left hanging to drip dry. They were then cut up into hams, shoulders and sides.

This meat was then placed in the smokehouse on shelves and packed down in plenty of salt for six weeks. After six weeks in salt, the meat was washed clean and hung up in the smokehouse to dry. We then took hickory or maple wood and built a smoking fire. This took a couple of days but it flavored the meat and it would keep all summer. Sometimes we would buy liquid smoke to put on the meat. After this process we wrapped it in paper until we needed it. This was the old way but it worked in our day.

Chapter Twenty-Four

Berkeley County hospital was ready for operation in 1932. This was the dream of Dr. William Kershaw Fishburne, who pushed hard for a medical facility locally. He persuaded a number of northerners who owned seasonal homes in and around the Moncks Corner/Pinopolis area, to match fund with local donations to get the hospital built.

Betty Brigham began her nursing career in this hospital when it opened and was there when it closed in 1975. She also served as a nurse during World War II in other areas.

The hospital was used as health center since it closed and is now scheduled for a 1.6 million dollar renovation.

'The City of Dreadful Night' is how the newspaper described the earthquake that hit Charleston, SC on the night of August 31, 1886. The earthquake also did damage in Berkeley County.

The Charleston jail was badly damaged and one Captain Kelly stood at the door, pistol drawn, holding back a mass of frightened prisoners. Thirty eight eventually escaped from the unguarded prison yard.

The city was wrecked with masses of fallen bricks, telegraph and telephone wires. The air was filled with people crying and praying. Spectators reported the mysterious sighting of a cross atop the main station house. An estimated 90 percent of the city's brick homes were damaged. Many of the old buildings have earthquake rods in the weakened and twisted walls to help hold them together to this day.

Charleston and the surrounding counties have seen a lot of pain and heartache over the last two hundred plus years, but have always managed to survive. I think it says a lot for the strong willed people who settled this area and begat many tough offspring.

Craig Lewis was about sixty years old when he got hurt on the job. He went out on disability and moved to another state, where he bought a lot and began building a new home.

One day as he was laying brick, a young man came up to him and began a conversation. They talked for a while and the young man stated, "You're a hard working man for your age." The old man enjoyed the complement and replied, "I am in good physical condition and can work most young men into the ground today." He didn't know he was talking to a private investigator who was sent to check on him since he was on disability. Within a few days he was told it would be necessary to go back to work, for he had lost his disability! He went back to work and stayed there until he was sixty-five years old.

Bill Gennings, Cash McCall, and Floyd Wright were avid night hunters in the Hell Hole Swamp area of Berkeley County. When this one incident happened, Bill drove his late model Ford truck to the area to be hunted. He had an errand to run so Cash and Floyd told him to pick them up in four hours. Bill was to look for a green bush in the road and they would be in the bushes nearby.

After a while, Cash and Floyd killed an old doe deer, put a green bush in the road as planned and sat down in the bushes to wait on their friend to pick them up. After waiting for a while, a Ford pick-up pulled up to the bush and stopped. Thinking it was their friend, they grabbed the doe deer up and put her in the back of the pick-up. Lo and behold the pick-up was driven by two game wardens! When the astonished game wardens realized what was happening they jumped out and tried to arrest Cash and Floyd. The two men, realizing they had put the deer in the wrong truck, headed for the woods in the d ark and got away. As the years passed they enjoyed telling the story and got many a laugh from it.

Ole Hiram Littleton says you will never have but one good friend and one good dog during your lifetime. As you grow old and the years begin to put a stoop to your shoulders, you may sit and reminisce about your past life, and there will always be one friend and one dog that will stand out above all others. Old Hiram also said if you are looking for a helping hand, look at the end of your shirt sleeve as this will probably be the only hand you will ever be able to completely depend upon.

Ash Rivers worked for the railroad and began racing pigeons. He would put several pigeons in a cage and ship them to Danville, Va. Someone there would open the cage and let them loose. The birds would return to their respective houses which had a time clock in it that would record the exact time they returned home. This went on for a while until ole Ash got deathly ill. His fellow workers found him one day sitting on the railroad tracks, crying. They thought he had had a nervous breakdown. After taking him to the hospital where they ran the necessary tests, the doctors found Ash had contacted some type of bird disease from the pigeons which affected his nervous system. The doctors did all they could for him but in a short while he passed away. I can't help but wonder when I go into someone's house with pet birds or parrots in it, if they really understand the seriousness of this bird disease.

This gentleman lived on a mountain and one day he had a visitor who asked to use the bathroom. This was back in the ole days and he did not have indoor plumbing. He told his visitors he didn't have a bathroom in his house. The visitor then asked, "Where do you use the bathroom?" He answered, "I use the bathroom all over the side of that mountain." Of course we all know this didn't happen in the low country. We don't have mountains around here.

Jane Creech said her family was raised back in the ole days when there wasn't such a thing as indoor plumbing, in her part of the woods. Her family was large so when she started taking a bath, she would start at her head and wash down as far as possible. Next she started at her feet and washed up as far as possible. When the boys left the room Jane would then wash 'possible'. It was difficult to find privacy back in those days if you had a lot of siblings.

Ole Yates Carmicle was in his eighties. His children were all married and gone and then he lost his wife. He had a mule he wanted to sell so I went to see him on a Friday afternoon. He said, "Yes, I'll sell the mule. Come back Monday morning and bring your truck." Sunday night I received a phone call from one of his daughters telling me her daddy had changed his mind about selling the mule. She said, "That is all my daddy has to come home to." I didn't go back as I didn't want to take his last family member from him.

Dink Smith and his wife Carrie, were on a trip to the upper part of South Carolina when they took the wrong road. After traveling quite a distance, Dink realized they were headed in the wrong direction. Irritated he had to turn around and go back the other way. Dink, angry with himself and Carrie, told his wife, "You should watch the road closer for me!" Carrie told him it was his responsibility since he was driving. This caused an argument and Carrie fell silent. As they were riding down the highway, tired and disgruntled, Dink saw a mule standing in a pasture by the highway. He looked over at Carrie and said, "Is that Jackass a part of your family? You're as stubborn as one!" She told him in her sweetest tone, "Yes, dear...by marriage."

This old lady who is a senior citizen says she has become a frivolous old gal. She is now seeing five gentlemen every day. As soon as she wakes up, Will Power helps her out of bed, then she goes to see John. After this, Charlie Horse comes along and stays for awhile. When Charlie Horse leaves Arthur Ritis shows up and takes her from joint to joint. After such a busy day, she says she is tired and glad to go to bed with Ben Gay! What a life!

She also told me "Old folks are worth a fortune with silver in their hair, gold in their teeth, stones in their kidneys, lead in their feet, and gas in their stomachs."

This gentleman said, "It's not the pace of life that bothers me but the sudden stop at the end."

Tim Wentworth was on his death bed and he knew he had done one of his neighbors wrong, many years before. He sent for the neighbor to come see him. They talked for a while and after the kind neighbor forgave him and started to leave, Tim made this remark, "Now if I don't happen to die, let's just leave things as they were!"

Ole Hoss Cantwell decided to become a preacher. He didn't have a license so he began preaching at the smaller churches. One Sunday as he was preaching at a little church, he began laying the bush down and told the congregation they had grown cold and were nothing but a bunch of 'mossy-backed hypocrites'. After church was over, two of the members of the church went outside and cut them a good stick. They were waiting on the preacher to come out of the door and when he did, they fell on him with the sticks and put a whipping on him. They changed ole Hoss' attitude and to my knowledge, he never spoke ugly to his congregation again.

Dave Dingle ran up a bill on credit at the country store and would not pay it. One day as he entered the store, he saw his name with the amount he owed, in the store window. Ole Dave hurried to see the magistrate and asked him what he could do to the store-owner for putting his name and amount of debt on display. The magistrate said, "My advice to you is to go back and pay your bill, then the store owner will remove your name from his window." He did this and they both lived happily ever after.

Lap Dixon and his friend, Brent Fields, went hunting on the hunting club land one day and somebody's yearling cow was passing through. They shot the yearling, loaded her in the trunk of the car and carried her home with them. After butchering the cow, they took her to a freezer locker to be kept for them until a future date. Lap told Brent, "I put half of that cow in your name and the other half in mine. You can pick up yours whenever you are ready." Brent told me he never did go back to get his part of the cow.

Ronnie Helton was caught putting arsenic in his neighbor, Victor Sprent's, water bucket. Victor had an old hand pump he used to get water for his family. Back then a bucket of water would be brought into the house and a dipper put into it for the family to use. Ronnie was angry with Brent for some reason and the arsenic was the way he planned to get even with him.

The magistrate was notified and a search began for Ronnie. Nobody had seen him for several days until my dad, who was a constable at the time, walked under a tree in the woods with low hanging limbs on it. Ronnie had taken pine boughs, laid them across one of the bushy, low hanging limbs, thus making a bed for himself. He was lying in this bed when my dad saw him and made him come down and handcuffed him.

This was late in the evening so my dad brought him to our home to stay until the next day.

The magistrate had an old model "A" Ford that was not very reliable and they decided it would be best to travel in the day-light hours. My dad chained him to the foot of the bed during the night and he was taken to the Moncks's Corner jail next day.

After spending several years in jail he was allowed to come back home. I talked with him several times afterwards and he said he had learned his lesson. To my knowledge, he never had any more problems and was a hard working honest man.

Peter Bullock owned a large farm in Berkeley County. One of his neighbors told me that Peter would plant one of his fields in corn and velvet beans. This was during open range and people allowed their hogs and cows to run loose. When winter came, he would open the gate and let any stray animals come into the field of corn and beans. He would then catch them and keep them for himself. Back in those days every man with animals running loose, had a mark they put in the animal's ear so they could tell their animals when they saw them. Peter allowed 'any animal with a hole under its' tail belongs to me.'

One man whom I will merely call 'Henry' operated a small restaurant back in the ole days. I knew him well and one day one of my friends came to me laughing his head off. He told me that he went into Henry's restaurant and didn't see him or any customers around so he walked into the back looking for him. He said he was surprised to find Henry standing near the kitchen sink full of dirty dishes, urinating on them. It was an embarrassing moment for both of them.

After World War II ended, I enrolled in a barber college in Greenville, SC. I stayed at a boarding house there. The lady of the house served meals in her home, but occasionally I stopped in at a local restaurant. I got to know the waitress real well and she informed me the manager would take left over bread from the customers plates coming back to the kitchen, grind it up and mix it in with his hamburger meat. This would stretch his hamburger meat a little further and he would get paid twice for the bread.

Chapter Twenty-Five

The depression began with the stock market crash in 1929. President Roosevelt was elected president in 1932. The president started the CCC's (Civilian Conservation Corps) to give young men work. They were paid thirty dollars a month. They stayed in the camps and worked in the woods. They had to dig ditches, build roads and set out young pine trees. President Roosevelt was elected again in 1936, 1940, and 1944. He died in office in 1945 before World War II ended. Since Harry Truman was Vice President he became our next president at Roosevelt's death.

On Dec. 7, 1941, Japan pulled a sneak attack on Pearl Harbor, resulting in the US declaring war on Germany and Japan. Germany had a lady called 'Axis Sally' who broadcast over the radio telling the American soldiers to give up and come on over to their side. Japan had a lady named 'Tokyo Rose' who did the same thing.

During this period of time our country coined a phrase as follows: 'A good Jap is a dead Jap'. Many Japanese-American families were put in camps on the West Coast during the war. The families who were victimized simply because they happened to be born Japanese, have, in recent years, been paid a large amount of money by our government. I'm thinking it was a small compensation for what they went through, though. I feel the worst part was the humiliation of not being recognized for whom they really were: Americans, just like the rest of us.

The 442nd regiment was made up of all Japanese-Americans. The highly decorated outfit served in Italy with the fifth army under General Mark W. Clark, during World War II. They proved themselves skilled, worthy, and true Americans in battle. I was told the Germans really feared to do battle with them. I knew several Japanese-Americans and they were good, honest, hardworking people and served this country well in peace time and during the war.

I was drafted into the army on my 19th birthday, August 4th, 1943. The other draftees and I left Moncks Corner, SC on the Greyhound bus. After arriving at Fort Jackson, we were taken before a group of doctors for a physical exam. We were then given a mental exam. After passing these exams, we were take to the barracks for the night. Locals, Reggie Salisbury and David Murray, were also there. The next day, my group was sworn into the U.S. Army.

We were immediately given three weeks leave, put on a Greyhound bus, and sent back to Moncks Corner. When the three weeks were over, we returned to Fort Jackson for assignment to boot camps. I was sent to Fort McClellan, Alabama for sixteen weeks basic training and then on to Fort Meade, Maryland to await transit overseas. Instead of leave I got ten days delay en route to stop by home.

We left Fort Meade, Maryland in march 1944 on a troop train going to Camp Patrick Henry, Virginia. From there we left for Norfolk, Virginia where we boarded a large troop ship going to Casablanca, North Africa. The ship carried 5,000 soldiers plus the navy personnel and some U.S. Marines. We were not in a convoy and our only defense against submarines was to travel in a constant zig-zag course. When I questioned the navy personnel about the timing of the turns, they told me that it took seven minutes for a German submarine to line up a torpedo on a target and that's why they changed courses every seven minutes.

After nine days at sea, we landed at Casablanca, North Africa. After a few days there we were loaded on a troop train and taken to Oran, North Africa. They called this train the 'Forty and Eight' as they said each box car was supposed to hold forty men standing up or eight mules. I know there must have been forty of us in my car for we were packed.

After arriving at Oran, North Africa, we were loaded onto a British troop ship and taken to Naples, Italy. We disembarked from this ship and were loaded in army trucks and taken to a tent city a few miles inland from Naples and there we stayed until we were called out for Front Line Duty.

Having trained with an anti-tank outfit, I was not called to Front Line Duty until after the Anzio Beachhead. I had trained on a 57 millimeter anti-tank gun that was mounted on wheels and pulled by an army truck. Upon contact with enemy tanks, we could cut this gun loose, spin it around and make ready to fire in just a matter of seconds. Since, strictly speaking, I was not then an infantry rifleman, I was held in reserve. I was probably very lucky.

We lost a lot of men at the Anzio Beachhead landing. A short while after this, they needed infantry replacements, not anti-tank soldiers. One Saturday afternoon, the commanding officer of the tent city began to call us all out in formation. They loaded us down with ammunition and live hand grenades, and there was little mistaking where we were headed. It made no difference now what M.O.S. (Military Occupation Specialty) number you had or what you were trained to do. They needed bodies for the front lines.

We were loaded in army trucks and taken as near the front lines as they dared go. We got off the trucks and started walking to the Front. It was scary as we were already under artillery fire from both sides. It was difficult to tell by the sounds of the shells overhead whether they were going from our artillery or coming from the enemy. After walking almost all night we were close to the front lines when daylight came that Sunday morning. We could hear the machine guns and rifle fire, and mortars began to drop their shells all around.

Then I found out about *mule trains*. Believe it or not, they did have *mule trains* in Northern Italy. One man would lead the first mule with probably a dozen or so others tied to the lead mule walking single file behind him. The mules had racks on their backs which would carry two five gallon cans of water or two cases of army rations. They used the mules at night to get water and rations as close to the fighting men as they could. It would be up to the men to get it from there.

I was told to follow one of these mule trains on my way to become a replacement in Company C, 361st Infantry, 91st Division, 5th army under General Mark Clark. I stayed with this outfit until the war ended and I found out all I wanted to know about what it means to shoot and be shot at by the enemy. I was fortunate to live through it without getting hurt seriously. Only twice did I come close to getting wounded-once when a piece of shrapnel hit my foot, giving me a hot spot on my leg, and another time when a bullet or a piece of shrapnel put a hole through the side of my jacket.

My outfit was in three battles or campaigns: Rome to the Arno River, North Apennines Mountains, and the Po Valley. We lived like rats. Older men with beards looked awful. One time we were on the front lines for thirty-three days without a bath or shave. They did pull us back behind a mountain for a few days, at this time, but we were under artillery fire nonetheless.

During all the maneuvering we sometimes got our lines mixed up, got behind each other or cut off part of each others troops. Once my outfit was surrounded and some of our men captured. Of course, some of the men I knew and fought with were killed in battle. In all this confusion of battle, we actually got face to face with the enemy, so to speak.

We moved into this town one night under cover of darkness and there were several men ahead of me. All of a sudden I heard German voices and I froze since I couldn't see them. We were moving up the sidewalk and I backed up against the wall. I could still hear them, even closer than before, but I couldn't see them. All that I knew was that I had to get some cover. A few buddies would have been nice to have around at the time, also. I felt behind me and eased along the wall until I found a door knob. I opened the door and to my surprise, there were American soldiers already in this building. These Germans realized we were coming in from this end of town and they began shelling us. We had one tank with us and during the shelling the men jumped out of the tank, left it running and came into the building with us. I heard one of our officers order them back to the tank and to return fire, but they refused to go. Sometime during the night, when things had gotten quiet, I realized the tank was no longer running. I assumed it ran out of gas.

When daylight came, the Germans decided to pull out. They had captured some of our men and one of them was our company medic. He got away the next day and made it back to us a few days later. He said he was in a truck convoy of Germans moving to the rear when the U.S. Army Air Corps spotted them. He said they began striking them and were doing a good job on them, so the convoy stopped and the Germans left their trucks and ran for cover. Our medic said he ran too, but in another direction. He, along with some of the other soldiers, got away. He came back to us with a small paper weight Swastika in his pocket as a souvenir. But souvenirs could be dangerous.

Another time we crossed a river and moved into a town. We had one .30 caliber machine gun with two men operating it. One of them had a souvenir P38 Luger, a German officer's pistol. The other one of the pair had taken it off the officer after he had killed him, but his partner had relieved him of it probably through gambling. We had a standing order not to get taken prisoner with such a souvenir, because the Germans would take it personally and probably summarily execute us.

At any rate we left these two at the edge of town to guard our rear. It was late in the afternoon and we didn't meet any resistance. We decided we would spend the night here as we were tired and needed some sleep and rest. There was an entire company here so my platoon took over a two-story building. We put two men on the front door to guard us so we could sleep.

In just a short while, as dark came upon us, so did the Germans. We had gotten behind their lines and cut off a tank outfit. When they found out where we were, they began to fire shells from their tanks into the buildings. They captured both guards from outside the door and began to call to us in good English, "Come out with your hands up."

The lieutenant said, "Hold your fire; we can't fight tanks with rifles. Let's hope they don't come in that door because, if they do, we have got to shoot it out with them."

It wouldn't have been much of a fight, a platoon of riflemen against a tank outfit. I ran up the stairs and looked out the bathroom window. The moon was shining brightly, glistening against the snow. I could see a German soldier moving around in back of the building hollering, "Come out with your hands up." I think I could have taken him, but I knew it would probably get us all killed. If they broke in the door downstairs and the fireworks started I had this German soldier all to myself. Strangely enough, our luck held out again. The Germans apparently did not have enough time to check out every building and they began to move on. However, the two guards on the door were taken, and we never again saw the two soldiers who had the machine gun and the souvenir P38.

My hat is off to the Air Corps. Once, when we were pinned down, our Company Commander called for help. They sent six P51 planes, and I was sure what they were, because they had red noses on them. They put on a show! They would take turns diving and striking the enemy right in front of us! It was good to know that, for the most part, anything flying overhead was ours. And we had other support. At times they gave us both tank and artillery support. But the Germans had very good artillery, especially their 88 millimeter guns. They were aces with their artillery as we learned from experience. If they put a shell above you and then one below you, you had better run as fast as you could, because the third shell would always be on target. If they ever got you in a bracket you knew they were going to blast you.

Once things quieted down at night, on the battlefield, both sides sent out patrols. We had to stay in touch with each other, and both sides would try to take prisoners to find out what the other was up to. On this fateful night I was one of the twelve man patrol sent out to capture a German soldier for interrogation purposes. We had just got a new Lieutenant, and he was designated to lead the patrol. He gave us the plan before we left. He figured, since we were in the Appenine Mountains knee deep in winter snow, we would do better moving very little. So he told us to go down in a draw and spread out to wait for the Germans to send a patrol through there and to us.

We checked the password with our forward dugout and moved on into the draw. However, we probably got too close to the skyline and the Germans must have seen us. In just a few minutes a shell landed a short distance above us. I turned to the nearest man and asked him, "Where did that shell come from?" About that time a shell landed a short distance below us. I said, "I know where that shell came from!" Then came the third shell, right on top of us. It killed the Lieutenant and wounded five others-six of the twelve of us, were down.

The concussion got me, and for a few minutes I couldn't get things right. Then I realized we had taken a hit and everybody who was able to run headed back to the dugout. I was right with them, regardless of my confusion! They put a shelling on the spot for a few minutes and then it was over. We ran back to help the wounded and found one

161

man with both legs shot up pretty badly. He was pulling himself along the best he could with his elbows. He cursed us for everything in the book because we ran and left him. He didn't stop to realize we would all probably have been killed if we hadn't run. We got the dead lieutenant and five wounded out of the area. The man with the bad leg wounds was an Italian-American by the name of Rudy Recupero from Chicago, Illinois. We got a letter from him after he was safely back in the states, in a hospital near his home. He had time to think about it and he wished us all well. I have never heard anything from him since.

Even before the Germans could see the end coming, they would relax some when we were waiting for a push. This may sound funny, but I saw the German cooks bring hot chow to some soldiers in a little valley below me, as I sat in an old bombed out building. We were in a holding position and did not want to give our position away. They would take showers right out in the open, not knowing but probably suspecting that we were able to see them. Some of the younger ones would even wrestle with each other.

I can recall one instance in the Po Valley in which we captured a group of German soldiers after a brief fire fight. We ordered them to throw down their rifles and put their hands behind their heads. One German soldier called out in fluent English, "Is there anybody here from New Jersey?" We had two men from New Jersey and they spoke up. One was a private and the other was a staff sergeant. The German soldier said he had an expensive camera in his bag and that it mounted on a tripod. "I know I will have to give it up, so I want you to have it." He then walked over to the sergeant and gave it to him with this remark: "I lived in New Jersey several years but came back to Germany and was caught in the draft. You are welcome to it."

In the spring of 1945, we were preparing for our last offensive which was the Po Valley Campaign. We were dug in just above a town called Bologna in the North

Appenine Mountains. On the day it began, the artillery men started with a barrage after barrage on the enemy in front of us. After pounding the enemy for a while, the shelling stopped and it was time for the infantry to do their thing. We moved out and hit the enemy with all we had. After a few days, resistance became weak. We put a twelve man squad of men on top of each tank and began moving faster. As we would run into spots of resistance, there would be a brief fire fight, and the enemy would put up a white flag or wave a white handkerchief in surrender. We would make them throw their guns in a pile and move to the highway, heading them to the rear. At first, we put an armed soldier behind them to keep them moving, but after a while we just disarmed them before heading them to the rear.

The Italians had switched sides by then, but the old Fascist leader Mussolini, was still claiming to be premier of Italy as he was at the start of World War II. He came under Hitler's protection, but the Italian people joined the Allies and kicked Mussolini out of power. They called themselves Patriots and one night they caught Mussolini trying to escape the country. He was shot and hanged upside down in the town square in a town in Northern Italy. The townspeople told me that they went by and spit on him. They left him hanging there all day.

After a time on the Front, they would pull us back, give us as much as three weeks leave in Rome, set up portable hot showers, an give us clean clothes.

Rome did not suffer any damage during the war. Germany and the Allies had an agreement to spare this city from any shelling or bombing. Rome is a city noted for its treasure of history, art, statues, and paintings. I went down in the Coliseum where lions were turned loose on Christians and gladiators fought to their death. I went up in St. Peter's Cathedral located in St. Peter's Square where the Pope addresses the masses.

163

During our three weeks R&R in Rome, I had a buddy named Sergeant Glee. One day we hired an old Italian man to ride us around Rome in his horse and buggy taxi. After the day was over, we went into the mess hall, got some canned good and a couple of army blankets to pay him with. Later on after returning to the Front, Sergeant Glee was killed. An enemy patrol infiltrated our position and he was shot in the back in his foxhole with an enemy burp gun.

After being in Rome for three weeks, drinking good wine and cognac and talking with the ladies, I had just about decided to stay in Rome, become an Italian, and let somebody else fight the war. I had seen enough horror to last me a lifetime.

The first dead man I saw on the Front Lines was an American medic. He had a red cross painted on his helmet with a red cross on his arm band. The Red Cross is recognized internationally by the Geneva Convention. They do not carry firearms as their job is to take care of the wounded. But he was killed anyway.

The first wounded man in our outfit was near me when shrapnel from a shell hit him in the upper chest. The medic had a hard time trying to stop the flow of blood. They finally got help and took him to the rear. I never saw him again. But sometimes men were lucky...and we could never explain that luck. When the artillery round knocked me silly, another soldier had been holding his collapsible machine gun, burp gun I called it, and the shrapnel tore the gun apart as it rested in his lap. *He* didn't even get a scratch.

It was the rule in World War II that if a soldier got wounded three times, he was eligible to be removed from the Front Lines. This soldier in my outfit got wounded the third time but refused to leave us. He was a large man, Mexican or Indian-American. One day as we were advancing against the enemy, I passed him lying in a crumpled position by a trail in the mountains, dead as a soldier can get. My thoughts were and are, on how he could have been safe if he had taken advantage of that rule.

Being pulled back from the Front was a joy to all of us. It was a time to relax, eat hot chow and have fellowship with out buddies. The sad part was when it came time to move back to the Front. There would always be several accidents in which a man would shoot himself in the foot, leg, or hand. Usually it would be their excuse that they were cleaning their rifles and had accidental discharges.

All of us faced that fear at some time-surviving all of the horror, sharing some sane time and then being asked to go back into the horror again. Sometimes it hit in the heat of battle. One day we were pinned down by a German machine gun and the Lieutenant called two men out from cover to order them to go knock it out of action. As we lay crouched close to the ground, these two men began making their way forward. In just a few minutes we heard a rifle shot and one of the men came running back to us with his hand bleeding. We knew what had happened, and the lieutenant looked at him and told him to head to the Rear until he found help. He told him so that all of us could hear that he had not heard the last of this: "I'm going to have you court martialed!" Yelled the Lieutenant. I never saw the man again.

The war in Europe ended but we stayed on duty in case we were needed in the Pacific. At the end of World War II in August, 1945, due to the dropping of two atomic bombs on Japan, we were ready to start coming home. Eleanor Roosevelt said, "Our boys overseas should be de-loused and checked for other diseases before returning to the states." Franklin Roosevelt's famous words were, "I hate war; Eleanor hates war; we all hate war." General Douglas MacArthur said, "I shall return," and "Old soldiers never die, they just fade away." During the Vietnam War, Lyndon Johnson was reputed to have said, "The American people never had it so good-two chickens in every pot and two cars in every garage!" He failed to tell the people how many boys were getting killed and wounded each week. I have always laughed at the way these leaders talk about war, but it's us privates who fight them. We see war a little differently from the way the 'big boys' do.

I ran into a British soldier in Rome who had written a song concerning the war. It made a lot of sense to me. He sang it several times. Here's part of it: "Here's to Lady Astor, we hope that she hears this, when she's on the Platform doing her famous twist, see the death white crosses some which bear a name, heart aches and suffering they have known, but now in death they slumber on."

President Roosevelt summed it all up in three words, when he made this famous statement: War is Hell." I saw a lot of things happen during my tour of duty on the Front Lines. Some things I don't care to talk about. I'm just thankful to the Almighty God that I made it back. Being retired I like to sit on my front porch early in the morning, sip on a cup of coffee, and reminisce about the past. I still don't know how I made it.

To all Americans, take a few minutes of your time to honor those who fell in Battle in order for each of us to be free. To all the young men that we left behind to sleep under those small white crosses on Foreign soil, I say 'thank you and we pray you did not die in vain'.

And I want the world to know: there are no atheists in foxholes! During my days on the 'front' I always carried a Bible that had a gold-plated metal on the front of it. My mom sent it to me. It was said the metal would stop a bullet. I don't know how true it was but I know there weren't many of us who didn't keep our Bibles close at hand. I remember an incident which happened in Florence Italy. A little girl ran up to me and gave me a picture of the virgin Mary for good luck. I still have that picture today.

With war looking us in the face now, I often think of the young man I was back then. I worry about the young men who are taking up arms to protect our freedom once more. I wonder if they are as scared and lonely as I was. It was a feeling impossible to describe to someone who has never experienced it.

The first atomic bomb was dropped on Hiroshima on August 6, 1945. The pilot who flew the plane that dropped the bomb, was Colonel Paul Tibbets Jr. The name of the plane was 'Enola Gay'. The first atomic bomb was named 'Little Boy'. Between 75,000 and 100,000 people were killed in this blast and 68,000 were injured.

The second atomic bomb was dropped on Nagasake on August 9, 1945. It was named 'Fat man' and killed approximately 70,000 people although it was a mile and a half off its' target. It was estimated that 250 allied soldiers were killed in this strike zone.

Harry Truman was president at the time and Jimmy Byrnes from South Carolina was secretary of state. Truman did not hesitate to give the order to drop the atomic bomb after it was tested in the New Mexico desert.

Had it not been for these two atomic bombs, it was estimated that approximately one million Allied soldiers would die before Japan surrendered. The date had already been set for Now 1st to invade Japan. The war was over in Europe and we were on alert to go to the pacific theater of operations.

On August 14th, the Emperor of Japan made a special broadcast to his people, telling them America had begun using an inhuman bomb and fighting now would be useless. He called for them to surrender, but it was not until September 2nd that the necessary documents were signed, making it official.

Chapter Twenty-Six

This chapter is devoted to Reginald B. Salisbury who was a Prisoner of War during World War II and told in his own words. "Once at a VA Hospital, somebody told my wife that her husband had it easy being a POW in Germany instead of Japan. She was terribly upset over the comment. If the story of starving, stated calmly by somebody who had come to a comfortable grip with the memory of the ordeal, is one of ease, then the audience must not have been listening."

"In the 40's, the service, much as it has during the course of time, offered an opportunity to make a better life. I was raised in the Ridgeville area on a chicken farm, and I quit school in the 10th grade. It was not long before my father sat me down for one of those finger-shaking, foot-stomping talks. It was about patriotism and realities: patriotism, somebody's got to do it! Realities-20 acres and a mule to make a living. One of my brother's had gone into the army, the other into the navy."

"In the summer of 1943, I was called to Fort Jackson. We were split up into groups of fifty. Mine passed everything one night, and the next morning when the whistle sounded we got out on our lines. That was the first time I ever paid attention to any Marine. They were the first to get their pick of recruits. Every tall, burly guy would be pulled up by the collar and jerked around a little and told by one of the Marine Sergeants 'You're now a marine!' Then a Navy man came up and asked for volunteers. He offered to put us up in a hotel in Columbia and feed us at a restaurant. I didn't volunteer for anything. The three of us who were left, went into the army."

"I did my boot camp at Camp VanDoren, Mississippi, where the brand new 63rd Division was built from the ground up. Our emblem was a flame with a blood dripping dagger through it. I was one of the first. Another recruit, the First Sergeant and myself were alone in the big camp. I have to admit even now that I was slightly intimidated by the empty, ghostlike environment, but when troops started coming in from the stockade and other unlikely places I was not any happier. I started volunteering for any assignment- Raiders, Paratroopers, anything to get out of there. I was turned down for all of them, but then an Indian named 'Half' and I got shipped out to Ft. Meade and on to Camp Miles Standish, in Boston and trained as scouts."

"The unit had about 100 scouts and the number went up and down from injury and illness. Most were well-educated Indians who spoke French or German. We trained at night and played during the day. For whatever reason, we got pretty lax treatment. No matter what kind of trouble we got into we always got off the hook."

"I had been in for less than a year when I got shipped out, March 12, 1944. I went in a cargo ship with no room below decks and no bunks. We slept on weathered decks, huddled in corners or out of the way places. It would be just over a year, May 14, 1945 when I got back to the U.S."

From Liverpool we were trucked inland to an area of clover fields and valleys. We slept in pup tents and spent time figuring out how to get to town at a time when passes were short. We resorted to gagging and binding the guards and slipping into town. As long as we would stay together, the MP's would round us up, pay for damages, and get us back to camp. If we staggered in alone, we had to pass through a Belt Line where we got framed pretty good.

As we moved for the progressive staging for D-Day, we came across different types of town. In one town, black and white soldiers were only allowed to come in on separate days. However both groups of soldiers would sneak in and out anyway and there were fights and even some fatalities. The local youth were in on it too, laying ambushes in the countryside at night.

I shipped out of South Hampton, spending the last few nights under guard in a fenced in area, the MP's serious about maintaining security and order just before the invasion. We were fed from thermos bottles passed out among us.

Sixteen of us scouts were shipped over on a shrimp boat. We were offered tranquilizers for our nerves, the only case of such an offer that I have ever known. I accepted. Dumped over the side in two man teams, we made the beach in rubber rafts. A British sailor spit tobacco juice between me and my Indian partner, dismissing us with,"You're on your last ride, you bloody blokes."

"Our job was to get behind enemy lines and find out what was going on. The Indians would send information back using Navaho language and the Germans couldn't figure it out."

"We were sent from outfit to outfit, changing so often that after liberation, I could not give an account of just who it was I was fighting with."

"In the hedgerows around St. Lo, there was terrible carnage. The tanks at first used the gates in the hedgerows, but the German anti-tank fire expected that. The carnage was as bad as that from gliders, landing in fields with spikes that tore into the planes. Tanks would roll over our own men and their bodies would stand up stiff like old road kill. The 29th Division had helmet insignia of half blue, half white dots. Many men caught a bullet in that circle until men learned to paint over them, rank insignia and other markers. Soldiers also learned never to raise up for a look in the same place twice."

"A man from Mullins came up with the idea of putting bulldozer blades on the tanks, and then the tanks simply dug up the hedgerow where they wanted to go and the break-out began."

"After that I went to the area of the 30th Division Operations and had the misfortune to come under the command of a 'green' officer, so green he was on the front lines still wearing his full pack."

"Across the valley that was the 'No-Man's Land' on my front, I could see two Germans consistently in the open. It looked like an obvious trap, but the green officer ordered a patrol led by my partner and myself. The patrol was able to get to some Germans in a house in a small wheat field. The officer, back behind the lines dismissed the fears of a trap and ordered the attack: 'Sting 'em!' The Germans were burned out some of them shot."

"However, Germans had surrounded our patrol and after a brief fire fight, we were out of ammunition. Able to get low enough so that the grazing fire did not kill us, we survived. The Germans starting barking out orders and one of the Indians translated the obvious, 'Come out with your hands up!'"

"One of our men had his ear drums ruptured by artillery blasts. I had been hospitalized with a severe reaction to poison vine. We both had insisted on staying in combat and now we were both POW's."

"On both sides, survival depended on who handled you. The ones who caught us made us look at the Germans we had just killed. I thought they were going to shoot us. Instead, we were searched and the Germans took all of the field jackets, cigarets, and chocolate. Hitler had outlawed chewing tobacco so I got to keep mine. Then we were ordered to march with our hands on our heads. If we got tired and dropped our hands, we got a rifle butt in the backbone. The long ride away from freedom had begun."

"The Germans did not have manpower to waste on guarding POW's. They left two men to guard the sixteen prisoners and a simple set of rules: if one tried anything we all died. For a period of time, while the Germans were retreating before the rapidly advancing Allies in France, we got food from the French we passed by. At times the Allied long range artillery actually bracketed the little column of prisoners."

"Once into Belgium, we joined others, all of whom were stripped and put into a big warehouse. Many of us still had invasion money. My little cache amounted to $100 in ten dollar bills. I had taken thread from my sewing kit and wound the money tight, thus able to get it past inspections."

"We were shipped across the country-side by rail. Horses came off a boxcar and many more than the load maximum of 40 men were stuffed into the car without so much as cleaning out the manure. It would be seven days before we got off. We had a 12 quart bucket of rolled oats to eat, a hole with barbed wire across it for air. When we pulled onto a siding, locals would pass in water, and we would have to fight off hoarders, to make sure an equal amount went to all. They put manure in a boot to use for a latrine, and the contents would be emptied through the barbed wire hole."

"When we stopped in Germany, I, along with several others, was segregated in interrogation rooms and grilled by a Japanese officer who spoke fluent English. Recognizing my Charleston accent, the Japanese officer and a German Naval officer grilled me especially hard, continuing to hammer me with information about the Charleston area which they had obviously visited."

"Giving only name, rank, and serial number, I incurred their wrath. It was off to the salt mines for me. That very afternoon I saw the first jet plane of my life. Two of them were in a dog fight with Americans in much slower but more maneuverable planes. One of the jets turned too slowly and plowed into a big brick chimney, exploding violently."

"Back aboard a train, Allied planes intervened. The locomotive was knocked out and the tops blown off of the POW boxcars. All of the POW's escaped death, but the train they loaded us into took us to Dachau, a notorious death-camp. Older men told us we were finished, but after two nights, we were loaded aboard another boxcar that had just turned out Jews. The stench and filth was the worst I had ever seen."

"From there I was shipped to Stalag 7A. I would like to remind people that the only thing that Hogan's Heroes television series got right, was the layout of the barracks. Everything else was stark survival."

"I consistently worked outside of the camp and it worked for me. Those who worked in the cities and villages of Germany had an opportunity to trade and scavenge for food and made out some-what better. We would ride the rails in to work. When trying to release the pain of dysentery we would simply hang our rear-ends out of the cars. Look-outs would tell us when it was clear, or else we would get whacked severely."

"We cleared rubble, delivered milk and potatoes from carts to the German people, patched roofs and repaired rails. Depending upon the guards, we sometimes even had a chance to feel like 'people', a dangerous indulgence. Once, ever the clown, I used my prized little piece of soap, not as big as the motel variety of today, to joke around with a Polish woman who was sorting mail. I offered her the soap for a 'a little loving' at which offer the German guard dropped his paper and began beating me. I laugh about it now, but would like to remind people that it wasn't a bit funny then!"

"There was little we could do about the filth. Our underwear and socks simply rotted off of us. The lice took up residence so we could lift our shirts and pick them off. Our pants remained soiled with the refuse of dysentery and the dirt of work."

"Sometimes the guards would rob us but at Stalag 7 we could get some relief. The commander had been a POW in England in World War I and he would remove any guard mistreating the prisoners. However, he could not protect us from the young SS men who might mistreat us at any time out in the work area."

"The SS men saved their energy for the Jews, for the most part. In the towns the Jews worked on the worst jobs, like carrying rail ties. They had cups tied to their stripe clothes and they would crawl through a line of SS men beating them, to get their pitiful little cups of thin cabbage soup, having to drink it, while under such duress."

"Close to the end of the war, I watched helplessly as a train sidetracked and simply rolled out its' cargo of Jews. Those still alive, some 360 plus souls, were gunned down and covered over. Being a POW was simply a matter of survival though, and it was after liberation that we were able to bring back Allies to recover the Jews' bodies."

"Being a POW was about food. From the beginning march, whatever we could get was important. In the march across France we ate little apples no bigger than a thumb. At the end of that march we were starving. At an abandoned mental institution we caught a rabbit. Possessed of some sense and dignity, we decided to cook it, but the only pot available was a chamber pot. After scrubbing it with sand and stream water, even burning it some, we still couldn't get rid of the stench. Finally we fired it really hot and hit it, knocking off all the agate and then we cooked the rabbit."

"It was there that a thin, tall kid from New York climbed a tree to rob his first bee hive, bringing down the top layer of honey. Bees stung our tongues and lips, but that honey was sure good!"

"Red Cross packages got in to us in the camp fairly often, but they were no great meals. They came in 18" square boxes about 10" high, and 16 men shared the saltines, spam, hard chocolate, cheese and tea bags. The Sir Walter Raleigh cigarettes were for enlisted; officers got better brands like Lucky Strikes."

"The men like myself who worked outside, would forage secretly or trade cigarettes and candy for dandelions, Polk salad, potatoes, barley and wheat. Meat like house-cats had been eaten by the Germans long before. In the early days we could get as much as 16 two-pound loaves of bread for cigarettes, but later were lucky to get a third of a loaf. We fashioned stoves out of cans and roasted the barley which popped like corn. Not able to clean greens or grain, we ate it all, dirt and stones included. The stones tore up our teeth but it was what we had to eat in order to live. The Germans gave us only a pint of soup a day and at the beginning a morning cup of something they called Russian tea. Eventfully the tea gave out and we only had hot water in the morning."

"When I was liberated, I weighed 97 pounds, but I survived. And the Germans were not much better off. When I rode the cart to pass out the potatoes and milk, I would break my chocolate into little pieces about the size of a little finger, wrap each one in paper and pass it out to the hungry German children who looked for and followed my cart. On a visit to Europe in later life, I was reunited with one of these same children in this small and ever changing world."

"As the end drew near, food, stability, and certainly, broke down. At different times we had been able to scrounge parts to make a radio, hide it, and listen to the news. We had some idea but the constant presence of American planes and the movement around us made us grow even more aware. That and the fact that the guards got older."

"Three weeks before liberation, I was working on rebuilding a rail line, but a P38 would take a picture, bombers would strike the next day and the roundhouse and rails wold be blown up and then we would start over again. Our bomber couldn't hit the bridge until the very end, and after that the project died out. It was here that the massacre of the trainload of Jews took place."

"Our last guard was in his 70's and too weak to climb steps in our last housing. I would hold his rifle while the old guard climbed the steps. When the Allies got close enough, we switched roles. The Germans asked us to tell the Allies they had been fair guards. They warned us to watch out for villagers or soldiers seeking vengeance. Generally we helped each other to liberation."

"The Allies cleaned us up and then began interrogating us. They were almost as bad as the German's. I was healthy enough to avoid a long hospitalization and I began to work my way home. Because of delays, I was able to enjoy a little freedom in Europe, although it would be a long time before I adjusted completely to being something other than a prisoner."

"My Indian partner and I, once again somewhat free, managed to get a motorcycle, alcohol and food and went to see the sites. The food we gave to the Germans and we got the use of a house in return. Later in Paris we got money from the government and rented a surrey for sight-seeing. But this was not what we really wanted. We wanted to go home."

"After 63 days home I went to Florida and got sent to Camp Gordon in Augusta for mustering out. I can sum up the rest of my life like so many of the other World War II GI's —with a simple and concise story. I got married, got work, made a career and retired."

"I have a good wife and a nice marriage. I do everything she tells me to do. That line is good for a laugh, but the real story is I could not tell my wife about being a prisoner. It was a part of life I buried for 30 years. On the night that the Vietnam prisoners came home in 1973 I told my wife that I wanted to watch the event on television. As the POW's came out of the plane, I was overcome! I stayed up all night telling my wife the experiences I suffered as a

POW. Since then, we have both been active in forming and actively supporting POW associations, making trips with others who shared the experience, and making that early tragedy another part of an American family's life."

Chapter Twenty-Seven

Ole Hound-dog Hatchet lived in our neighborhood and it was said he would steal a nickel off a dead man eyes! One day Jack Pierce lost a goat so he went to ole Hound-dog's house and asked him if he had seen his goat. Hound-dog said "Yeah, I have your goat but I've already butchered him. I'll share with you though, if you'll be so kind as to come in and let by-gones be by-gones." They divided the goat and both men were happy.

This gentleman had a neighbor that was hard to deal with on many occasions. He nicknamed him 'Hemorrhoids' as he said they were both a pain in the butt.

Wick Garrison was talking with a stranger in Moncks corner one day, telling him how many deer he had killed out of season. The stranger asked him, "Do you know you're talking to a game warden?" Wick replied without batting an eye, "Well, buddy, did you know you are talking to the biggest liar in town?"

This gentleman fell into a whiskey vat and drowned. He was cremated and they say he burned for three days.

Mike Morrow loved this song and used to sing it in the old days. I will give it to you as follows: "You are bound to look like a monkey when you grow old! I can tell by your hair, you have got monkey blood somewhere and you're bound to look like a monkey when you grow old. I can tell by your face that you came from the monkey race and you're bound to look like a money when you grow old. I can tell by your knees that you have been climbing coconut trees and you're bound to look like a monkey when you grow old. I can tell by your feet that you don't smell too sweet and you're bound to look like a monkey when you grow old. I can tell by your nails that you have been hanging by your tail and you're bound to look like a monkey when you grow old. Yes, you are bound to look like a monkey when you grow old!"

This gentleman was a senator from SC for many years. He was up in age when he married for the first time, a young pretty thing. He lost her after several years of marriage. He then married another young lady and they had several children together. When asked why he married such young women, he remarked, "I would rather smell powder and paint than Sloans liniment."

Jesse Walker was stopped by a highway patrolman for speeding. The patrolman noticed Jesse was not wearing a seat belt and he began writing him another ticket. Frustrated and angry, Jesse started talking ugly to his wife. The patrolman asked her, "Does your husband always talk to you in this manner?" She said "Only when he is drinking!" The patrolman wrote Jesse a third ticket for driving under the influence of alcohol.

A Math Lesson: He was teaching her arithmetic, and he said it was his mission, he kissed her once and kissed her twice and said, "Now that's addition." And as they added smack by smack in silent satisfaction, she sweetly gave his kisses back and said, "Now that's subtraction." Then she kissed him and he kissed her without an explanation, 'til smiling they both kissed and said, "That's multiplication." But then her dad came on the scene and made a quick decision. He kicked the lad three blocks away and said, "That's long division."

Back in the thirties, we had a blimp come over our neighborhood flying low and slow. On the side of the blimp were the letters, 'US'. We had never seen one before and it was rather scary. Some of the people saw the letters 'US' on the blimp and they said "That spells *us*! That thing is coming after us!" Many began to run and get inside their houses. We laugh about it now, but it wasn't funny at the time.

Reckless Martin ran a grocery store back in the ole days. He had a glass showcase where he kept a good supply of candy. On top of the showcase, he glued several nickels, dimes and quarters. On occasion customers would come in for candy, and try to steal the change. Of course it would not come loose. The customers would then look at the store-owner very sheepish, realizing they had been caught trying to steal. Reckless told me he got many good laughs from this practice.

Out House Jokes and Other Crap: This gentleman says Bill Clinton is the joke of the nation. He has taken what we find in the outhouse and brought it into the White House.

This gentleman says he wants to be dead and in heaven at least thirty minutes before the devil finds out he has died.

This gentleman says when he dies he wants to be cremated, this way he would be one up on the devil.

This gentleman said "During the depression we all had to wear clothes with holes in them. One time I put on three pairs of pants and you could still see my ass."

One friend of mine said every time he looked up his family tree, a gorilla took a crap in his face!

A man I once knew said "All a woman is good for is to keep count of the children and chickens." I don't think he lived to be very old.

This gentleman says, "if you have a friend, use him but don't abuse him."

This gentleman told me during his time in the Navy, he saw a big fat sailor use the bathroom, but he couldn't find any toilet tissue. The large man got up, pulled up his pants and made the remark, "Very well, I'll catch you next time!"

This gentleman told me he was courting his girl friend one night at their house when the clock struck twelve. She said, "It's twelve o'clock and nothing said, you go home and I'll go to bed!" She was expecting to hear the 'magic' word as she wanted to get married.

This gentleman said, "You will never succeed in drowning your sorrow with alcohol because sorrow knows how to swim."

This gentleman told his son to go find a chair and sit down. He did but told his mother, "On the outside I am sitting down but on the inside I am standing straight up."

The statue of a general was given a chance to speak after many years and he was asked, "If you could move again, what would you do?" His answer was "I would kill 20,000 pigeons!

This gentleman was walking down a mountain trail one day when he met a mountain lion face to face. Not having a gun, he decided to kneel and pray. As he was praying, he looked around an saw the lion kneeling beside him. Relieved, he told the lion, "I'm sure glad to see you're praying too!" The lion said, "I'm not praying, I'm just saying grace!"

This gentleman was up in age when he committed a serious crime. He was hauled into court to face the judge. The judge sentenced him to prison for 135 years. This gentleman says, "Your honor, at my age there is no way I can make that much time in jail!" The judge said, "Boy, just do the best you can!"

During World War II, somebody came out with a song 'There's a gold Mine in the Sky'. The next day, 50,000 men joined the air force.

This gentleman says, "I know marriage is made in heaven but so are lightning and thunder!"

This gentleman says, "I would like to marry a woman who can cook, sew, clean fish, and paddle a boat. I would also like for her to have a nice bank account!"

This gentleman says, "The difference between a recession and a depression is: a recession is when your neighbor is out of work. A depression is when *you* are out of work!"

This gentleman says, "The fear of the Lord is the beginning of wisdom!"

This man died and went to Heaven. He had three surprises waiting on him. He was surprised to see people there whom he didn't think would make it, then he was surprised some of the people he thought would be there had not made it, and mostly he was surprised he had made it, himself!

This man died and went to Heaven. An angel escorted him to a cabin and told him, "This is your home!" He said, "Angel, I was always told I would inherit a mansion when I got to Heaven." The angel said "Well, you didn't send anything up here to build a mansion, so you must settle for your little cabin!"

These two men were invited to sing for a revival service at a very small one room church. They accepted the invitation although they had never been there. The first nights' service was going good and they were singing high praises when they saw a man come in with a box full of rattlesnakes. The two men lost no time asking the snake-handling pastor, "Where do you want the other door, for we are getting ready to leave here."

Preacher Stanton was getting ready for services on a Sunday morning. As usual there were about as many outside as there were inside the church. He came to the front door and invited everyone inside, then made this remark, "Those of you chewing tobacco, just take it out of your mouth and put it on the stump over there. I will personally guarantee you no hog, dog or any other animal will bother it." Then he made his way to the pulpit and started service.

This same preacher was holding service at a church and his brother-in-law came in and joined the congregation. After a lengthy service, his brother-in-law decided to leave. As he got up and started for the door, preacher Stanton said,

"Some people come to the church with a small bucket so I guess my brother-in-law's bucket is already full!"

A preacher I am acquainted with went over to Russia to hold a revival only three blocks from Red Square. There were ten ministers over there working underground, passing out Bibles and holding services. They all met on this night in an old building to plan their work. The KGB raided the building and lined them up against the wall presumably to be shot. The KGB then said, "If you don't want to be shot, renounce your religion and leave." Seven ministers left. The KGB said, "Now that we have got rid of the phonies, let's have church!"

Hambone Alderman says back in the depression years he attended school faithfully but most of the time he had no lunch to bring. The luckier children brought lunch from home and while it might not be much at least they had *something*. Hambone decided one day he was tired of being hungry and watching everyone else eat, so just this one time he would just steal someone else's lunch. But...Hambone had been taught right from wrong all of his life, so if he was going to do this, then he must do it right. He stayed in during recess while the other kids went out to play. He picked up every lunch bucket and weighed it in his hands, savoring the luscious meal he would find. Finally he decided on the heaviest one. When lunch time came he hurried outside, the stolen bucket in his hand. He found a nice place by himself and shut his eyes for a moment thinking of the feast ahead of him. His mouth watered with delight and his hands shook in anticipation. *After all I am just a little boy... I shouldn't be held accountable for every sin I commit*, he thought. He took the lid off of the bucket. There in front of him was a *hammer and two hickory nuts*! He *never* stole anything again.

Clyde Mills, like the rest of us, had only an out-house during the depression years, for indoor plumbing was almost unheard of back in those days. Clyde's children said they knew where he was going when he went by the barn. He would pick out two red corn cobs and one white one. When asked why, Clyde replied, "If I use the red corn cobs first and then the white one, I can check the white corn cob to see if the red corn cobs have done their job!"

Chapter Twenty-Eight

Leland Kennedy said the old Sears Roebuck Catalog was a luxury in the old days. When you went out to the little house behind the big house to do your business, you could scan through the catalog and maybe find a toy or piece of clothing or something you wanted to order from Sears, while you sat on the seat. When you were finished with your 'job' you could use a few pages of the catalog for wiping your 'necessary'. Toilet tissue was a scarce item in the old days.

Ben Holbrooke says you were born with two ends: one to think with and the other to sit on. Heads, we win and tails, we lose.

I once heard an old granny say, "Had I known my grandchildren would be so much fun, I would have had them first!"

Ben Holbrook had a lot of good sayings up his sleeve. One of my favorites: "The only way for some people to wake up with a smile on their face is to go to bed at night with a coat hanger in their mouth." Unfortunately he's right!

Ole Holbrook also was reported to have said: "Me and my wife live in a two story house. She has her story and I have mine!".

This preacher told me about the time he pulled up behind a little lady at a red light. It changed several times and the little lady just sat there like a bird dog pointing a covey of quail. She kept watching the light but did not move.

So the good preacher says he first started biting his nails and then he began beating on the dashboard with his fist. Finally when he could stand it no more, he rolled down the window and hollered at the little lady 'Granny, either move it or lose it!' He got right ugly, he said! He didn't realize it but a car load of people from his congregation had pulled up alongside of him. They just smiled and waved to him. Right then and there he started praying to God to give him patience.

Garrad Fillmore went up before a conference board to get a license to preach. He said he felt the 'calling'. After the Bishop asked him some questions and he gave the right answers, the Bishop asked to speak to Garrad's wife. The Bishop was reported to have asked Garrad's good wife, "Do you think your husband is qualified to preach?" She replied to him, "Yes sir, all he wants to do is lie on the couch, watch television and eat fried chicken."

These two highway patrolmen stopped a car for speeding near Hebron, SC. They began writing a ticket but neither of them could spell 'Hebron'. One officer said to the other, "Let's turn him loose and catch him again when he gets to 'Lanes'. I can spell that one!"

A soldier was on k.p. duty while in the army. The inspection officer was coming for dinner so the soldier made some pies with crust on top. Usually a cook will take a fork and press the edges of the pie. The officer looked at the pies and asked the soldier what he used to press the edges of the pies. The soldier replied, "I have a set of false teeth I use for that sir." The officer then asked if he didn't have another tool in which to use on the pies, the soldier said, "Yes sir, but I use it to make the hole in the middle of the pie." I really can't swear to the truth of this one.

During the depression years in the 1930's, the government would send a large truck with cloth bags filled with surplus food to be distributed in different areas where the people were having a hard time getting the necessities of life such as food, clothing and shelter. When the food was finished the people would then use the cloth sacks to make clothes for the children. All bags were printed with 'not to be sold' on them. Now Abigail Helton was a rather hefty woman and she was a good seamstress. She used the 24 lb flour sacks to sew any necessity she might need. One day at a church picnic, she was sitting on a ditch bank with her dress pulled a little high. Brent Norwoods' little nephew was just learning to read and he was also just learning a few facts of life, so he peeped at the sight of Abigail's bloomers sticking out from under her dress. He read the words out loud for everyone to hear, '24 lbs... of the... very best...not to be sold'.

One of my classmates wore a skirt made from a crocus bag that she had dyed green. If she hadn't told us we would never have known it.

I graduated from high school in 1941 and lunch was only two cents a day. We had a struggle to get one thin dime to eat lunch for a week.

President Roosevelt started the Work Projects Administration (W.P.A.) during the depression. This gave a lot of people work to help them support their families, although it was only fifty cents per day. There were always men hanging around the work-site looking for a job in case one of the workers did not report for work for some reason. There just weren't enough jobs for the people so they could only hire one man per family at best.

This old fellow had a few laying hens and a rooster during the depression. His wife went to pick up the eggs one evening and there were no hens to be found. The old rooster was in the chicken house with a note tied around his neck. She caught the rooster and read the note. It said, "Lonesome papa; thanks for the hens!"

After the stock market crash in 1929, the banks closed up and people lost their money. This well known gentleman went to the bank to get his money. He held a shotgun in one hand as he tapped on the door with his other hand. Somebody in the bank cracked open the door to see who was there and he pushed his gun barrel through the opening. They could not shut the door so he made his way into the bank.

He told the employees, "I'm not here to rob or take any money. I have a large amount of money in this bank and I want every cent of it." They counted out his money and he left. I was told he was the only man fortunate enough to get his money out of the banks.

Paul Morgan took his teenage son with him to church when this ole ugly man came into the church for the service. The boy kept looking at the ole man and finally asked his dad, "What's wrong with that ole man?" His daddy thought he would give him a good answer so he made this remark, "Lightening struck him!" In a few minutes the boy tapped his daddy on the shoulder and asked, "How many times?"

Aaron Smith got into an argument with his neighbor and his neighbor slapped one side of his face. Aaron told him, "The Bible says to turn the other cheek, so I'm turning the other cheek, but after that, the Bible didn't leave any further instructions. I'm free to do to you anything I want to, so you had better watch out, Bubba!"

This preacher from St. Stephens stopped during his sermon one night and made this remark, "Some people remind me of hogs, always looking *down* in their food containers and never looking *up* to see where the food is coming from!"

A pastor was having a problem with his ministry at a particular church. He decided to leave. As he preached his last message to the congregation, they noticed a piece of mistletoe hanging down from his coat tail. After finishing his message, the preacher started for the door. Quietly he turned to the congregation and said, "If you don't like my ministry, you can kiss under the mistletoe because I won't be coming back."

This missionary from our little town in South Carolina had been over in Africa for a long time. Upon returning to New York harbor, she looked at the statue of liberty and said, "If you ever see me again you will have to turn around as I don't ever plan to go back."

188

Jack Knowles was taken to the old Berkeley County hospital to have some tests made. The nurse brought him a cup and asked him to get a specimen for her. After she left, someone brought him a cup of apple juice. Before he could drink the juice, the nurse was back and she said, "Oh, good, I see you have already got my specimen for me." Jack replied, "Yes, but let me run it through again as it may be better the second time around." He took the cup of apple juice and drank it right down. The nurse, thinking he had drank his specimen ran out the door and didn't come back. Jack said he really got a good laugh after pulling this joke on her.

Haney French always said, "If you see an ugly kid on the street just follow him home and you will find two more ugly people."

Haney also said, "It used to take a bale of cotton to make a woman a dress, but now a silk worn can do it on his lunch break."

Haney was on a roll when he gave me this recipe for a long lasting marriage. "Never let the sun go down on your anger and remember, the rosebud is beautiful but you have to go through a lot of thorns to get to the rose."

This gentleman told me that he had found a way to get ahead in life. "Don't pay any of your old bills and let your new bills get old."

This gentleman said, "I started out with nothing and I still have some of it left."

This gentleman said he could remember when bootleggers had to wear badges to keep from selling corn whiskey to each other.

Anna Belle Jones had a daughter who was thinking seriously about getting married so Anna Belle gave her this advice, "Choose a husband like you walk through a cow pasture, 'very carefully'."

This gentleman was discussing with a friend the way prices were going up on everything. "But here is one consolation: women's panties are still coming down," He said in all earnestness. The man listening to the conversation made this remark: "Not around my house!"

These two old gentlemen were discussing why a male hog had tits. They finally agreed that if he ever gave birth to a litter of pigs he would be able to nurse them.

This gentleman says back in the W.P.A. days, during the depression, one drop of sweat from one of those workers would cure any disease.

Cecil Cornett says he was twelve years old before getting his first pair of shoes, during the depression. "The roads were all dirty and kept in shape by a road grading machine. When this machine would grade the roads near our house, I put on my shoes and walked backwards in the fresh plowed dirt for several miles just to see my shoe tracks."

Someone told me this piece of news recently: He said these three young boys were playing with a piece of rope near the highway when President Clinton came along and ran off the road into a lake of water. They hurriedly threw one end of the rope to the president as he was drowning. President Clinton caught the rope and the boys pulled him out.

The president said, "Boys, you saved my life and I want to repay you in some way. Each of you make a wish and I will pay any amount of money to make your wish come true." The first boy said, "I would like to go to Disney World." The president said, "O.k. your trip is paid for, so enjoy yourself. The second boy said, I would like to fly on a large jet airplane. The president said, "O.k. your wish is granted." The third boy said, "I would like to be buried in Arlington National Cemetery." The president said, "Son, you are awful young to make that request so I must ask you why?" The boy replied, "Mr. President, when I go home and tell my daddy I saved your life, he is gonna kill me!"

This gentleman says the weather had been so dry around his house that he had fish six months old that had not learned to swim yet!

Ole Frank Mettleton had several friends who made a lot of noise when they got together to talk. One day he stopped them and complained, "You people make more noise than two peg legged men in an ass kicking contest!"

Alonzo Clark married a real pretty girl and his friends kept asking him how he managed to get her for his wife. After being questioned for quite a while, he finally told them, "She was a little bit pregnant when I married her but not enough to hurt!"

This gentleman was walking around with his fly unzipped. A lady noticed and called it to his attention. He said, "Well, did you see my Cadillac in there?" She said, "No, but I saw your volkswagen with two flat tires!"

Harry Peters went to the Social Security office when he turned sixty-five to apply for retirement. He had everything he needed except something to officially prove his age. The lady told him, "You have to have proof of your age!" The man pulled off his hat and showed her his grey hair. She said "That's not enough!" He pulled off his shirt and showed her the gray hair on his chest. The woman said, "Not enough!" the man went home and told his wife what had happened. His wife told him, "You go back and unzip your pants! They will give you your disability!"

Bonnie and Betty, two old ladies that I knew, went to a strange town looking for a certain building. After criscrossing town several time, Bonnie said to Betty who was driving, "I think we're lost!" Betty replied, "Not me! I'm never lost as long as I have a full tank of gas!"

When seat belts first came out Suzanne Helton was involved in a car accident. The highway patrolman investigating the accident asked her if she had been wearing a seat belt. Suzanne said, "No sir, but I had my girdle on!"

Tray Hartman was asked by a judge in a court of law why he found it necessary to strike his wife. Tray told the judge, "I needed her to turn loose of me! She had grabbed me by the utensils!"

This gentleman said he could remember when love lasted a lifetime but things have certainly changed recently.

Uncle Pierce said some people lack ambition. "All they want out of life is a loose pair of shoes and a warm place to use the bathroom."

This lady went to her family doctor as she was getting rather large. The doctor pulled out his health charts and showed her that she was about seventy five pounds overweight. She then told the doctor, "According to the weight and height charts I'm not overweight! I'm just six inches too short!"

This skinny lady asked me this question, "Why is a fat woman and a moped so much alike?" I told her that I really didn't know but I would like to have her answer. She said, "Everybody wants a ride but nobody wants to be seen on top of one!"

This lady had a sick mule so she called the vet. The vet was eating supper so he told her to give the mule a dose of mineral oil and he would come out to her farm the next day. She asked him how to give the mule mineral oil and he told her to use a funnel. She then said "The mule might bite me." The vet said, "You are a farm woman. You should *know* about these things. Give it to him through the other end!"

The lady couldn't find a funnel so she used her Uncle Bill's fox hunting horn. After she had properly attached the horn to the mule's rear end, she reached up on the medicine shelf and got a bottle of turpentine by mistake. She poured the bottle of turpentine in the horn and it went into the mule's rear end. The mule raised his head with a jerk, let out a bray, reared up on his hind legs, knocked one side of the stable down, cleared a five foot fence and started down the road at a mad gallop. Every few strides the mule took, the horn would blow as the mule was getting rid of some gas.

All the dogs in the neighborhood knew when the horn was blowing it meant Uncle Bill was going fox hunting. They fell in behind the mule and everyone headed for the inland waterway. The bridge tender heard the horn blowing and figured it was a boat on the way, so he cranked up the bridge for the boat to get through. The mule and the dogs went overboard into the river. The mule drowned but the dogs were able to swim out without too much difficulty. Thus ended the life of a sick mule.

Troy and Tina had been married for many years. One day they were discussing their many years of life together when Tina made this remark: "Honey, you never tell me that you love me anymore!" Troy was surprised, "I told you when I married you that I loved you and if I ever changed my mind, you would be the first to know!"

These two gentlemen were discussing how mean this old fellow in their community was. One gentleman told the other, "I would rather sand paper a lions rear end than tangle with that fellow!"

Paul Clemmons was dating a girl by the name of Sharon Simpleton over in Georgia during the depression years. Paul lived in South Carolina and didn't have a car so he had to walk or hitch hike when he went to see Sharon. As time passed, Paul and Sharon decided to get married. They were married in Georgia and were walking to his home in South Carolina. After walking for quite a while without getting a ride, they decided to sit down on the ditch bank to rest. As they sat talking he noticed how large her feet were, so he asked her how she managed to have such large feet. She said, "Honey, that's caused by walking in that red Georgia clay." He told her without blinking an eye, "Sweetheart, I certainly hope you haven't been sitting in it!"

Clyde Booker was having some health problems so he went to see a doctor. As he entered the doctor's office, the nurse asked him what kind of insurance he had. His answer was, "I have fire and theft insurance." The nurse said, "I think your theft insurance will cover it!"

Carson Beal was a tough one. He served twenty years in prison. The day of his release he stopped in a restaurant this side of Summerville, SC, for lunch. This was during the hippie movement and a long haired 'hippie' sat at one of the tables. Now ole Carson sat down and began staring at the boy with the long hair. The hippie got up and walked over to Carson and with a sarcastic whine asked him, "Why are you staring at me?" Carson didn't miss a lick as he replied, "Twenty years ago I went to prison for raping a buffalo and I was wondering if you are my son!"

A bus driver and preacher died at the same time. The bus driver inherited a mansion but the preacher was put in a shack and wanted to know why. He was told, "You put a lot of people to sleep with your preaching but the bus driver drove so reckless he kept people praying all the time!"

Art Noe said he loved his wife so much that he would just pack up and go with her if she ever decided to leave him.

Art also said, "It is better to keep your mouth shut and be thought a fool than to open it and remove all doubts."

This gentleman says to help your children turn out well, spend twice as much time with them and half as much money.

This gentleman says the most sensitive nerve in a man's body is the one that runs into the pocket book.

John Smith bragged that he had landed a job which put him over approximately five hundred people. I found out the truth! He was cutting grass in a large cemetery!

Todie and Amber were traveling together and they decided to stop in this restaurant to have lunch. After lunch they went to the bathroom using separate stalls. Todie called out to Amber, "How do things look in your stall?" Amber answered her, "It's so filthy in here that I'm standing on the seat!" Todie called back, "It's no use standing on the seat because the crabs in this town can jump fifty feet."

Mark Hepplewhite said he knew all about waterbeds before the waterbed craze came into existence. He came from a large family and slept with four of his brothers. He said the water flowed freely during the night and he certainly slept in a waterbed!

Bubba said three of his friends ran off a bridge in a pickup truck. One was driving and the other two were in the back. The driver got out as he rolled the window down and swam to safety. The other two drowned since they couldn't get the tailgate down.

Doctor Fields had a patient with multiple personalties. After treating her for a while he decided to charge her for group therapy.

These two cannibals saw a man riding a bicycle in their neighborhood. One cannibal says to the other, "Here comes meals on wheels!"

Nort Jenkins said that he finally got to do something he had anticipated doing all of his life: flush the commode while flying in an airplane over the state of Mississippi.

What is this: the maker doesn't want it, the buyer doesn't use it and the user doesn't see it? A casket.

This gentleman was getting up in age when one of his friends brought him two caps which he wore proudly. On the front of one of these caps was a picture of a truck with this slogan, 'Old truckers never die, they just get a new Peter-built'. On the front of the other cap was the picture of a smiling egg with this slogan, 'You would smile too if you had just got laid.' We enjoyed many good laughs from these picturesque caps and the senior citizen who wore them.

A senior's lament: Thought I'd let my doctor check me, cause I didn't feel quite right. All those aches and pains annoyed me and I couldn't sleep at night. He could find no real disorder, but he wouldn't let it rest. What with Medicare and Blue Cross, it wouldn't hurt to do some tests. To the hospital he sent me, though I didn't feel that bad. He arranged for them to give me every test that could be had. I was fluerscoped and cystoscoped, my aging frame displayed. Stripped I lay upon an ice cold table while my gizzards were x-rayed. I was checked for worms and parasites, for fungus and the crud. While they pierced me with long needles taking samples of my blood. Doctors came to check me over, probed, an pushed and poked around. To make sure I was living, they checked me for sound. They have finally concluded, results filled many a page, what I have will someday kill me, my affliction is 'old age'.

Ten commandants of Love:1. Put your spouse before your mother, father, son or daughter. Your mate is your lifelong companion. 2. Do not abuse your body with excessive food, tobacco, drink or any foreign substance. 3. Remember that cleanliness is a virtue. 4. Willingly share all your worldly goods with your mate. 5. Do not forget to say, 'I love you'. 6. Approval of your spouse is worth far more than adoring glances from all the people in the world. 7. Keep your home in good repair. It will be a joy to you in your old age. 8. Forgive with grace because we all make mistakes and need forgiveness. 9. Honor the Lord your God every day of your life. 10. Do not let your business or hobby make you a stranger to your spouse. The most precious gift you can give is your time.

Friday the 13th: Fear of the number '13' dates back many years ago. The superstition is well rooted in history based on a study of ancient calendars. Tradition has it that on Friday the 13th, these things happened: Eve tempted Adam with the apple. Noah's Ark set sail in the great flood.

A confusion of tongues struck at the tower of Babel. King Solomon's temple toppled on the 13th.

When Northern Europe was converted to Christianity, a Goddess was banished to a mountaintop and labeled a witch. It was believed that every Friday she traveled in a carriage pulled by 13 black cats to a meeting with eleven other witches plus the devil, a gathering of 13. For many centuries after this episode, Friday was know as the Witches' Sabbath.

Chapter Twenty-Nine

Bootleggers and Corn Whiskey Stories: during the depression years, jobs were scarce and a lot of Berkeley County men were involved in making corn whiskey for a living.

Ralph and Tom were in the illegal (bootleg) whiskey business. They kept a bucket full of big head shingle nails in their car. When the revenue agents got behind them, they would try to outrun them but if this didn't work, they began throwing out the nails. In just a few minutes the revenue agents' car would be out of business with flat tires.

Late one evening ole Ralph and Tom took a car load of whiskey to Florence. After unloading it, they decided to rent a room in a hotel for the night rather than make the long trip back home. Now Ralph was a large man weighing over 300 pounds. After getting to bed he began some heavy snoring. Tom told me later "There was no way I could get to sleep so I started thinking how to stop Ralph from snoring. I reached over and caught his nose between my thumb and forefinger, thereby cutting off his air. When he began to jump and buck, I lay back on the bed, and pretended to be asleep. Ralph woke up and shouted at the top of his lungs, 'Wake up! Something's wrong with me!' I asked him 'What are your symptoms?' He said 'I'm having trouble breathing.' I told him, 'You have symptoms of a heart attack! I've been told you should never lay down in this situation! It would be better if you sat up in a chair!' Ole Ralph got up and sat in a chair all night long while I got a good nights sleep on the double bed." Tom always enjoyed telling this story.

Casey Hildrabrande was heavy in the moonshine whiskey business. He went around the Hell Hole Area and bought up all the moonshine whiskey he could find. He had the railroad install a spur track at McBeth that would hold two box cars. When one box car was loaded Casey would have his men pull it out and replace it with an empty one. In this way his loading operation was never stopped. Some of the boxcars of illegal whiskey were shipped up north to the gangster, Al Capone.

Bootleggers were always having problems with each other as well as the law. There were fights and shoot-outs almost every week. Often the problem was caused when they stole whiskey from each other.

A friend told me that during the depression he and his brother came across a moonshine operation in Berkeley County. They had a large number of cases of moonshine whiskey stacked up ready to haul. For some reason no one was around to guard it. My friend said they loaded all they could in their old car. It was so heavy it barely got out of the woods. They made out money wise but had they gotten caught, my friend would probably not have been around to tell the tale. Bootleggers don't take kindly to people stealing their whiskey.

Ira Putney was a sly ole fox when it came to making corn whiskey. He would set up his still and run whiskey until he had quite a bit made. Then he would take the still down and hide it until he sold all the 'shine. Ira used a copper upright still and he made some *good* stuff. He had every stump hole around his place full of two quart jars of corn whiskey. To my knowledge the law never did catch him or find his operation. He kept a bunch of hogs in the woods and I think they stayed drunk on his sour mash most of the time. I suspect they didn't have any problems with worms.

Paul Potts and his brother-in-law had a good operation going with moonshine and was doing good financially until Claude Cornett began coming to their still. They started to worry that Claude would tell somebody and the revenue agents would come in and tear their still up. They decided they would have to do something about it.

One Sunday afternoon Paul and his brother-in-law made their plans. When Claude came to their still, they caught him and tied him to a tree. They took some rags and soaked them in gas, placed them around Claude's privates and set him on fire. Now that is one terrible way to treat a person! Ole Claude lived through the ordeal but I was told he was left with permanent damage.

Two men were in the bootleg whiskey business and they decided to rig up a smoke screen on their car to use when the revenue agents got close behind them. They put it to use one day down below Jamestown on an S curve. The revenue agents were running them hard so they turned on the smoke screen. As the smoke began covering the road, the agents couldn't see. Their car left the highway and hit a tree. All the agents were all killed. I was told by an elderly man in Shulerville that he could show me the tree but didn't remember the names.

I kept asking questions until I came in contact with an old gentleman who gave me some of the details. He said, "I helped build the smoke screen, in the back of a garage in Moncks Corner." He told me they rigged up a bucket of burnt motor oil under the hood of the car which would pour onto the exhaust system when a device was pulled under the dash. This would cause a heavy smoke to come out from the rear of the car.

He said, "I will *never* give you any names so please don't ask me any more questions!" Since I talked to him, he has passed on, taking the names with him forever.

Elwood Garrison told me his father was a 'big time bootlegger' but attended church on a regular basis. Elwood was about fourteen years old when his father had him stay home on Sunday to sell whiskey, while the rest of them went to church. Elwood made a mistake. He sold two cases of moonshine to revenue agents. That was the end of Elwood's daddy's still. Elwood said, "I'll never forget the whipping my father put on me that day."

Harry Lewis was a smooth operator. He was a logging man and bootlegger combination. He would buy a tract of land to cut the timber and then he would move in his crew to make corn whiskey. He used the old 'Bob tail' trucks to haul his pulpwood and whiskey. He used short blocks on each side of his truck thereby creating a storage area in the middle of the flat bed. He would then stack cases of whiskey in this area and put 5 foot blocks of pulpwood over the load to cover everything from front to rear. Harry would then take his logging chain, pull it across the entire load and tighten it down with a jack. There was no way to see the whiskey and he could take the load anywhere without being stopped by the lawmen. To my knowledge, he was never caught. Some bootleggers used a dummy gas tank under their car to store the whiskey. They would cipher the 'shine out when they got to their destination.

Dexter High told me how he and his brother would fill half pint and pint bottles of corn whiskey and put them in suitcases. They would catch the 'boll weevil' train in Jamestown and go to Charleston over the weekend. Standing on a street corner, they would soon sell all of their whiskey within a short time. The next day they would go back to Jamestown unless they decided to stay over and have a bit of fun in Charleston.

John Joseph told me of the time he was helping his uncle Jackson make whiskey. The federal men had one agent that none of our local boot-leggers wanted to race with on foot. One day he got behind John and the race was on. He said he was doing all he could until this agent grabbed him by his coattail. John said "I left my coat in his hands as I came out of it. I found another gear I didn't know I had!" He managed to get away. He considered himself a lucky young man, for had he been caught he would have spent time in jail.

A man we called Dash loved to make and haul corn whiskey. I was told by a reliable source that he would load his Lincoln town car in Berkeley County and make a run to Florida. He did this for quite a while until one night he stopped at his usual destination to be unloaded. He went in and sat on a bar stool and ordered a drink. As he sat there drinking, three men walked up and surrounded him. One of the men said, "We know who you are, where you came from, and what you are doing here. We are not going to bother you now but let this be your last trip or you will be in serious trouble!" Dash took the men at their word and didn't go back.

Freight-Train Williams raised a family of seven children and never worked on a public job. He had a nice one-horse farm which he worked with diligence. He also had grapevines from which he picked the grapes to make wine. He had customers from all over the county who came to buy his homemade wine. He had about twenty-five hives of bees from which he got honey to sell on the side. Freight-Train's grape wine and moonshine operation was real profitable back in those days and he managed to live a good quiet life although he was checked out several times by revenue agents.

I've heard Freight-Train when he came to town on business, bragging how he had made whiskey all these years without being caught. He said the federal government should pay him a pension since he had put in over thirty years making and selling good whiskey.

He kept his moonshine whiskey in the living room. His wife was a rather large woman and she wore these old time, long, baggy dresses. When the law came to their house she would sit on the cases of whiskey and sew on her sewing machine.

Freight-Train also opened furrows with his mule and turn plow. After putting jars of corn whiskey side by side in the furrows, he would then take his mule and turn plow, and cover them up with dirt. When a customer came, Freight-

Train would uncover a jar, pull it from the furrow and take it to him.

Harold Moody was an operator of a fire tower in Berkeley County. He could climb up to the top an see for miles around. When a fire started, he would notify the forest service and they could move their men and equipment to any area, fast. These fire towers served their purpose in this era of time. One time Harold suffered a burn out and lost his home while he was operating the fire tower. He had a family and nowhere to go. Fortunately the old schoolhouse near him was vacant and he made arrangements to move his family in there.

I talked with one of his boys a couple of years ago and we discussed the burning of their home. He told me while his father was operating the fire tower, there was a large moonshine distillery operating in the area. The revenue agents blew up the still, leading the bootleggers to believe Harold had turned them in.

The family can't prove it but they believed their house was burned in retaliation for the still being blown up. The son joined the navy in order to send an allotment check to his mother. They were good people but put in a financial crisis after losing their home.

I was told there were some dirty tricks pulled on buyers who came to Berkeley County looking for moonshine whiskey. Tracy James was one of the men who outsmarted the moonshine handlers...once. Tracy had made a deal with a buyer for a huge sale of corn whiskey. He planned to make a lot of money on this deal. The bootleggers always used two quart jars, twelve to the case, to put their whiskey in. He filled his jars full of plain water but had his sample jar ready for the buyer as it was customary to sample the whiskey before loading it. The buyer took a drink. It was good 'shine and they made the deal.

The buyer paid ole Tracy James off in cash money and left the area. He had no idea he had bought a load of plain well water. Tracy went into hiding for a long time afterwards because he knew he was in serious trouble if the buyer found him. The men in the illegal whiskey business did not play games. Several men were found floating in the river or with concrete blocks tied to their feet.

I knew a lot of people involved in the whiskey making process and they were good trustworthy people who liked the thrill and fast money. I could get 120 proof whenever I wanted it. You could pour some on the ground, light a match and put to it and it would burn almost like gas. This was potent stuff and kept worms from growing in your stomach.

Making moonshine whiskey really put Berkeley County on the map. I would like to stress that in my opinion, in most cases, these were good men making whiskey to support their families during the depression. Anyone who came through the depression years (1930's), knows what I am talking about. Those were lean years and children needed food and a roof over their heads.

You can still see a lot of old shallow well spots in some areas where they got water to make corn whiskey.

I stopped at a whiskey still once and a large woodrat was eating away in a barrel of sour mash. I think he was drunk and he acted like he would attack me. I left him where I found him and moved on. I didn't buy any whiskey that day.

Old man Underwood had a twelve barrel moonshine distillery set up on US forest land. Vincent Craig, who was my friend, worked with him in the operation. Vincent told me that one day his instructions were to go to the still and put one tablespoon full of Red Devil Lye in each barrel to help make it ferment. For some reason Vincent got off balance and dropped the whole can of lye in one barrel. He became worried since so much lye in one barrel would probably kill the people who drank the whiskey. Vincent began thinking what he should do. Old man Underwood was older and tougher than Vincent. He knew he was in serious trouble if he told Underwood what really had happened.

Put under such enormous pressure, Vincent decided it best to turn the barrel of sour mash over and let it pour out on the ground. He went back to his partner and told him, "There was a bunch of hogs in the area and they turned over one barrel of mash before I could clear them out!" The old man cursed the hogs but didn't say anything to Vincent. Vincent said he went to bed with a clear conscience, knowing no man would get sick or die from drinking the bad whiskey and also knowing he wouldn't get his own head beat in.

During the early fifties, the revenue agents got strict on the moonshine whiskey making operations. They used a cub airplane to spot the stills from the air and had a ground crew in a jeep, notified by radio, to come to them with dynamite to blow up the still. The men operating these stills would run out of the woods when the airplane began circling the woods. They got in their cars and began riding the roads. They made sure they were nowhere close to a whiskey still when a raid was going on.

As the revenue agents got tough on the moonshine operation, some of the men who continued to make 'shine, often did not use the old method of all copper outfits, instead they began using large zinc coated wash tubs and car radiators in their operation. In one area of Berkeley County, men would frequently be found lying on the side of the road or in some corn patch, dead as a door-nail. I was told the deaths were most likely caused by drinking moonshine whiskey made in car radiators which still had antifreeze in them. As anyone knows antifreeze is a deadly poison.

Clyde Morton enjoyed the moonshine whiskey business. He used fast cars to outrun the revenue agents. He paid to have the cars 'souped' up and he told me he could do one hundred and thirty-five miles an hour. Clyde was tall, lanky and he had a bony frame. The sheriff told me one time to look at the front seat of Clyde's car, on the driver's side and I could see two holes in the seat where Clyde's 'cheek' bones had rubbed holes in it.

One gentleman ran a two barrel whiskey operation in his smokehouse just a short distance from his home. He had water lines running from his house and he heated with gas instead of wood. In the old days most people cooked with wood and the Revenue agents looked for smoke as well as the smell of sour mash in the air. This particular magistrate would ride the roads early in the morning, stopping at regular intervals to sniff the air. This was the best time of the day to smell a whiskey still. When the dew falls at night, the odor from sour mash fermenting at a whiskey operations increases quite a bit. I was told the good magistrate collected fifty dollars for every illegal still he turned in to the revenue agents.

Chapter Thirty

More 'shine stories: One man had a whiskey still located near his hog farm operation. When he was through with the sour mash he would feed it to the hogs. In this way he was getting paid twice for his corn. We all know the odor from an area where you raise hogs will override the smell of a whiskey still operation. I don't recall him having any problems with the law for they simply didn't smell a thing illegal.

People were pretty clever in our neck of the woods when it came to finding ways to hide their moonshine stills. One man had his moonshine operation underground. He built steps so he could go down in his cellar and make whiskey. Over the top of the steps he built a small building which resembled an outhouse (privy). Who on earth would ever think to look down an outdoor toilet for a whiskey still?

The revenue agents brought in an agent they had heard about from Georgia to help them catch some of our local bootleggers. It was reputed the agent was fast on his feet, and didn't get outrun by too many moon-shiners. Now Mick Johnson and Troy Helton had them a good moonshine still right near the Cooper River. Mick and Troy never were too smart. They were high on shine one day and while tending their still they made up a song. It went like this: "We have got a still on Liberty Hill and the revenue agents can't catch us!" To their surprise, this fast-running agent was hiding in the bushes listening to them. He jumped out and caught one man, handcuffing him around a small tree. He took off behind the other man who headed for the Cooper River. This man was an ex-lifeguard and being in the water was like throwing a rabbit in a briar patch. The revenue agents followed him for a way but had to turn back. When he got back to the man handcuffed to the small tree, he had gotten loose and gone. The agent did his best but to no avail.

This same agent got behind one of our local men at his still and the race was on. He told me he ran along fences that he could jump with ease but the agent had to find a fence post to help him get over the fence. After jumping back and forth across the fences a number of times, he got ahead of the agent and finally lost him. The agent got a good look at him and identified him later. He was sent up the river for one year.

Clipper Fields told me he had a buddy, Ernest Hemp, help him make some easy money. He would sell a load of moonshine whiskey to a buyer and leave the area. His buddy, Ernest, would be waiting farther up the road. He had a siren under the hood of his car. As the buyer passed him, he would take off behind him with his siren screaming. The buyer, thinking Ernest was the law, would pull over to the side of the road. Ernest would pull out a badge, tell the buyer to unload his whiskey and leave the area or go to jail. The buyer would do as he was told and leave. This trick was pulled on several buyers before someone finally caught on.

Art Clindinny says he didn't get much education in the ole days. His family was involved in the moonshine whiskey business. Art said since there are twelve two quart jars of corn whiskey to the case, he learned to count to twelve by counting them when he put them in cases.

Lew Garrison made and sold good corn whiskey. During the summer months, he planted sweet potatoes by the ole dusty road going to his house. As the vines grew long covering the roadside, Lew would hide his whiskey under the potato vines. We could pull up by his potato patch, blow the horn and he would come to us and ask, "How many jars you boys want?" We would tell him and he would reach down in the potato vines, pull out as many jars as we wanted, hand them to us and we paid him cash money. To my knowledge, he was never caught by the law.

I was told by one of the old timers that back in the depression a hardware store in Moncks Corner had a special post installed in back of the building to make copper coils for the moonshine whiskey customers. They would take copper tubing and wrap it around the post as many times as they needed to get the length of coils they needed. This way they could get a perfect coil every time without any bends in it. A good coil was necessary in any whiskey making operation.

Vern Smith was in the illegal whiskey making business and he was one slick old fellow. When a customer came by for some whiskey, he would get in their car and ride to the designated spot, get out of the car and walk backwards across the dirt road. Vern would get the amount of whiskey his customer wanted and then walk his tracks back to the car. Vern once told me, "That puzzled the revenue agents as all the shoe tracks were coming out of the woods and none were going in."

Bill and Mark were in the moonshine whiskey business. They had a big operation going and could deliver large amounts of 'shine anywhere. They sold whiskey wholesale to some of their customers who would then sell it retail to *their* customers making a good profit for themselves. They also sold whiskey on credit to some of their wholesale customers.

As time went on one of their wholesale customers, Vince Gilbert, got way behind in his bill. Bill and Mark tried to collect but Vince would not pay. Disgusted, they quit making deliveries to him. They got their heads together and figured out a way to make Vince pay. They got one of their friends to hire Vince to do some farm work. After setting a date, their friend notified them. On this day as Vince was fixing fence, Mark and Bill ambushed him. They put a whipping on him and took his wallet which had a considerable amount of money in it. Then Vince was put in their car and taken to a sandy area of Berkeley County. He was given a shovel and told to dig his own grave, a hole straight down as he would be buried standing up instead of lying down. After this hole was dug they put him in it and filled it in with sand until it came up under his nose. They left him enough space to breathe and kept him in this position all day. That night they dug him out and took him home. They told this man if he went to the law, they would be back and they would finish the job this time and then burn the house down around his family. I was told this story by Mark many years later and I believe it to be true.

This gentleman was in the moonshine whiskey business for many years. He bought this oldsmobile rocket fixed up with air lifts in the rear to accomodate heavy cases of 'white lightening'. He had it souped up so it would run 135 miles per hour. He could outrun the federal agents every time. After he got out of their sight, he would pull off onto some obscure dirt road and literally leave his pursuers in the dust. He was never caught but one day a federal agent got close enough to him to recognize him later. This agent made a case against him and he was sent to prison for one year.

After the year was up, he started wearing a badge as a constable. Our senator helped him get a presidential pardon from President Jimmy Carter. He then attended the criminal Justice Academy in Columbia. After about twenty years as a constable, he retired and since then he can be seen around town drinking coffee and talking with his friends. He is still healthy and loves to have fun.

Bull Milsap was in the army and traveling by Greyhound bus to a new army base. His bus stopped at a station in Chicago, Illinois where they had about an hour's layover. Bull decided to walk up the street to a bar and have a couple of drinks. As he sat at the bar drinking, he was idly looking over the different names on the bottles of whiskey. He saw one bottle that had the initials B.C.C. on it. He asked the bartender what B.C.C. meant, since he had never heard of it. The bartender told him, "You wouldn't know anything about that but it stands for 'Berkeley County Corn' which is illegal moonshine whiskey shipped up here from Berkeley County, South Carolina."

Bull was shocked to find moonshine from his hometown had made it all the way to the big city. He told the bartender, "I know all about Berkeley County Corn since I was raised in Berkeley County. I have never seen it advertised as B.C.C. though. Why, I am here to tell you, I cut my teeth on tops from jars of Berkeley County corn. I've drunk many gallons of it when I was growing up. We all drank moonshine whiskey instead of bonded whiskey since it was cheaper and a hell of a lot better!" The bartender was really surprised to meet a man from Berkeley County and especially one who knew all about the illegal moonshine whiskey trade.

Gale Whitmore told me he was in charge of some controlled woods burning in Berkeley County. When they were told to burn near ole Shep Wollard's house, well, Gale was a little worried. Shep was heavy in the moonshine whiskey trade. As Gale took his crew into the woods, all he could see were cases and cases of two quart jars of whiskey setting all around, under every bush. Gale was undecided what to do. A fire would break all those glass jars and probably blow up half the county with all that shine! And if that wasn't enough ole Shep would probably shoot Gale or at best give him a whipping he would never forget.

So Gale finally decided the only sensible route was to spread the word he was going to burn these woods and if anybody had anything of value in there he would suggest that it be moved. He went on to another area to do some burning and later came back. Old Shep had gotten the word and had hurriedly moved the whiskey. Gale was able to do his job without any more problems.

211

I heard someone say Old Clint Everest had a pond of water near his house where he stored the good corn whiskey he made. He was not caught by revenue agents, for they never suspected they would have to wade in a pond of water to look for jars of 'shine.

Dam-it Wilson was the son-in-law of the largest moonshine whiskey dealer in Berkeley County in the old days. He told me his father-in-law had a restaurant built in Berkeley County to serve as headquarters. The living quarters were in the rear of the building along with rooms for their out of town buyers to spend the night. It is reputed that Al Capone spent some time there.

Dam-it also told me that he worked for the state highway department and a law officer that he knew rode a motorcycle which led convoys of cars loaded with moonshine whiskey out of the Hell Hole area of the County. Another gentleman who lived in Berkeley County told me that there were many occasions that he saw a convoy of cars loaded with moonshine whiskey come by his house in broad daylight.

Bill Crissman operated a business in Monck's corner. Will Phillips worked for him when he was a young man. One day three men dressed in pin stripe shirts drove up in a big fancy limousine and parked out front. One of them carried a brief case which Bill later found out was loaded with cash money in large bills. After a short time they left, and ole Crissman came out of his office and made the remark, "Al Capone is the most honest man I have ever done business with." Will said he knew Crissman was in the illegal 'shine business on the side, but he was surprised he admitted it to him in such a casual manner.

Ike Henry told me that during world war II when sugar was rationed, it was hard to get enough sugar to run a still. He said he made a small fortune on the black market with his connections to get sugar and jars, which he sold at a huge profit. He said later he turned all the money he made into a legal business.

Ben Maloy had trouble getting sugar for his moonshine operation. He decided to use home-made syrup instead of sugar. It wasn't as good but he was able to stay in business until the war ended and then he started using sugar again. He said a man never had to use a laxative when he drank 'shine made with syrup.

Ole Ben worked the bootleg whiskey trade about all of his life. He told me about the time when he come up missing some of his jars of whiskey. He said for several weeks after loading up his cases, he would find several gone when he came to haul it out and deliver it to his customers. He finally got tired of it and loaded his shotgun and hid in the bushes near his still. In a short while a good friend of his came to the still, took a jar out of one of the cases and as casual as could be, he smelled and tasted it. Ole Ben said he had planned to shoot the b... who had been stealing his 'shine, but changed his mind when he saw who it was. Not that he minded shooting his 'friend', but the man was pretty high up in politics and was sure to have people who would find Ben and put him out of business and send him to jail. Instead ole Ben fired his gun a couple times over his 'friend's' head and the man left there running hard. He knew he had been caught so he didn't come back to Ben's still anymore. Ben said he often saw the man after that but he never mentioned the incident and neither did Ben.

Dab Jones was a local bootlegger and he had a wife named Charity, who could make corn whiskey better than he could. He loved to drink and he would get drunk and pass out so she learned their operation. She would haul the wood, fire up the pot and make the whiskey as he lay drunk. It was dang good whiskey too!

Al Smalls made corn whiskey about a mile from his house. His still was located down an ole woods road behind his house. He would load his mule and wagon with the necessary supplies, start his mule and the old mule would follow the road to the still. There would be a man at the other end to unload the wagon, load it back with cases of whiskey and start the mule back home. This trick evidently worked for he was never caught by the revenue agents.

One man I knew by the name of Jasper, had a mule trained to walk a logging road from the highway to his still. He had a rack made to fit on the mule's back that would hold sugar and jars to go *to* the still and would hold two cases of whiskey coming *from* the still. The mule would jump in or out of a truck on command.

When this gentleman quit the bootleg whiskey trade, I was able to buy the ole mule. She was the best plow mule I ever had the pleasure of putting a bridle on. When plowing you could tell her 'gee' or 'haw' and she instantly obeyed. At the end of the row all you had to do was tell her to come around. She knew exactly what you wanted her to do.

When thinking about this mule, I am reminded of two men I worked with years ago. One man told the other, "I can train a monkey to do your job and I think I would prefer the monkey."

Mick Fodder said he received a letter through the mail requesting a donation. It read as follows: "Dear Mr. Fodder, we have the distinguished honor of being members of a committee to raise 50 million dollars to be used for placing a statue of Bill Clinton in the Hall of Fame, in Washington, D.C. This Committee was in quite a quandary about selecting a proper location for the statue. It was deemed *not wise* to place it beside George Washington, who never told a lie, nor beside Franklin Roosevelt, who never t*old* the truth, since Bill Clinton could never tell the difference.

After careful consideration, we think it should be placed beside the statue of Christopher Columbus, the greatest dealer of them all in that he started out not knowing where he was going and in arriving, did not know where he was and on returning did not know where he had been and he did it all on borrowed money.

The inscription on the statue will read, 'I pledge to Bill Clinton and to the National Debt for which he stands, one man expending with graft and corruption for all.' Five thousand years ago, Moses said to the Children of Israel, 'Pick up your shovels, mount your asses and camels and I will lead you to the Promised Land'. Nearly 5,000 years later Roosevelt said, 'Lay down your shovels, sit on your asses, light up a camel, this *is* the Promised Land'. Now Bill Clinton is stealing your shovels, kicking your asses, raising the price of camels and taking over the Promised Land'.

If you are one of these Citizens who is not operating a legitimate business, are participating in the graft with money left over after taxes, we will expect a generous contribution from you for this worthwhile project. Sincerely, The Committee." Mick swore he had the letter and offered to give me a copy, should I need it.

John Kent had a nice race horse. He enjoyed riding and placing her in all the local horse races. She was always a winner so he told his son they should place her in the Ky. Derby as he thought she could win it.

His son decided he would load the horse up and head for the Kentucky Derby. His father couldn't go so they came up with this plan. Immediately after the race the son was to send his father a telegram telling him if the horse had won the race. To save money, John told his son to just abbreviate the words as he could make them out if he only used the first letter to each word.

After the race was over, the son sent his father a telegram with these words and letters. 'Dear Dad, ssff. Your son.'

John read the telegram and interpreted it as follows, 'started second, finished first'. He couldn't wait for his son to get home. When his son made it home he was very excited that his horse had won the race and he expected a nice big check. To his surprise his son said, 'No Dad, ssff mean she started and stumbled, farted and fell. No win and no money.

Clarissa Smith had collected a lot of pennies. One day she decided to wrap some, take them to the station and buy some gas. She thought it would be best to first ask the attendant if he would accept pennies. In her nicest Southern voice she said, 'Would you mind taking *pannies* for my *gas*?' The stunned attendant said, 'No, I'll give you the gas if you need it, but you can keep your *panties*'.

So much for Southern Sweetness.

Fred Morris had a band of gospel singers and it was always a pleasure to be with them in a church service. One day he got a call from a church in the state of Georgia to come there for a singing on a Friday night.

He told us he got his group together, loaded their equipment onto their old bus and headed out to the church in Georgia. It was located quite a ways from our small town in Berkeley County, SC. Fred and his group had never been there before so they had a difficult time trying to find it.

After many wrong turns and a lot of praying, they finally found the church. Seeing the bus from SC, the pastor came out and introduced himself. Apologetically and with a lot of smiling, he told Fred there would not be a singing there that night as a big time football game was scheduled and they would have to call off the singing.

After going this long distance and not being able to sing, they had lost time and the expense money which was usually made up for them at the end of the night. When Fred was visiting at our church one day, he told of the trip and he said, 'I despise a lying preacher!' Our retired conference Superintendent was there and with a twinkle in his eyes, he asked Fred and his group to sing, 'I Don't

Regret a Mile That I've Walked for The Lord.' I doubt Fred did much complaining after such a set-down.

I was out riding with a friend one day and we decided to stop by this home that had crossed a Jackass with a Zebra. This made a beautiful colt with the markings of a Zebra except the colors were not as bright as breeding a Zebra to a Zebra. While we were there looking at this colt, an ole buzzard with a broken wing came up to us and started pecking at my friend's shoe laces. It made me a bit nervous. I asked the lady what a buzzard was doing in her yard and she said 'He came here with a broken wing and I've been feeding him. He has made his home with me.'

I told my friend after we left that although I am not normally superstitious, I would not want a buzzard pecking at my shoes. I believed this to be a bad omen. Buzzards usually feast on dead things.

We're both still living though, so I guess it wasn't a bad omen after all.

I have heard that a good politician has got to be able to speak out of both sides of his/her mouth. The Indians referred to it as being able to speak with a forked tongue.

Back in the old days, Berkeley County had men that would treat you with 'love' and the utmost 'respect' in order to get your vote. If it didn't work, they would offer you money or do a personal favor for you. Then if this didn't work, they would threaten you and tell you that you were going to lose your job if you didn't vote their way. I was told by old timers some of the crooks took names off of tombstones in the cemetery and signed them on the voter register book. This was before accurate records were kept.

The majority of our politicians today are *probably* good law abiding citizens although I must say I certainly don't trust all of them.

A city boy moved to the country and bought a mule from an old farmer for one hundred dollars. The farmer agreed to bring the mule to him the next day. The next day the ole farmer drove up and said, 'Sorry but your mule died last night'.

The city boy said to the farmer, 'Just give me my money back'. The farmer answered,'I can't do that as I have already spent your money'. The city boy replied, 'Ok. Just bring me the dead mule and I'll raffle him off to get my money'. The farmer was shocked, 'you can't raffle off a dead mule', he told him. The city boy says, 'You just watch me. I won't tell anybody the mule is dead.'

Several months later, the ole farmer met up with the city boy and asked him what happened to the dead mule. He told the farmer he had raffled the mule off without telling anybody he was dead. He said he sold five hundred tickets at two dollars each and made a profit of nine hundred and ninety eight dollars. The ole farmer then asked if any one complained. The city boy answered 'Only the guy who won, so I gave him his two dollars back.'

Chapter Thirty-One

Gamewell Brown was a good friend of mine and he was a character! He was raised in Berkeley County and he knew all about the ole days, the good parts and especially the bad parts. As long as I have known him he has been a snappy dresser, usually clad in straw hat, starched white shirt and tie, with dress trousers and well-shined shoes. Anyone who knew him would tell you he was a very meticulous man. Until his death, he made a daily visit to the Huddle House in Moncks Corner to visit with friends and to tell anyone who cared to listen, one of his endless fascinating stories. Brown owned a little farm and he sold a car or a piece of real estate on occasion, from his home. He had been a welder at the Charleston Navy Yard, and he served the Air Force during World War II. In later years he worked as a constable for a while. But by far the most colorful part of his career was when he was in the boot-legging business.

He recalled hearing about the mobster Al Capone visiting Berkeley County to check on his illegal whiskey operation, when Brown was a child during Prohibition. He remembers when rival bootleggers shot it out on Main Street, one day in 1926 after a train blocked traffic across the tracks.

"They were all the time quarreling," he said, "Then they went to shooting and killing. Everybody made a little liquor back then," Brown recalled. "Much of it was done in Hell Hole Swamp where me and my nine older brothers and two sisters used to go by horse-back-riding and picnicking," he reminisced, "Now they call it Shulerville."

"The man who told me of Capone's visits actually worked for the infamous gangster. He told me that he received shipments of 'red' whiskey from Cuba, along the banks of the Santee. He then stored the illegal liquor in a man-made cavern close by and when the time was right, trucked it over to a railroad siding in McBeth. After it was loaded into a freight car, the whiskey was then covered up with a layer of lumber to disguise it for the northbound trip to Al Capone's Chicago," Brown said.

Later, during World War II, Brown was stationed at Shaw Air Force Base outside of Sumter. He was notorious with his friends for bringing back 'shine from his visits home.

Eventually he got into running bootleg liquor to Mullins, Marion and elsewhere along the back roads of South Carolina. Most of the time, he was just out of reach of the law.

"The state Police at the time didn't have nothing to run as far as chase cars," Brown said. But there was a federal agent out of Atlanta, by the name of H.PL. Clary, who did.

Clary got close enough to get Brown's license number several times and he would ticket him later, but ole Clary never did catch Brown in a car chase or foot pursuit, according to Brown. Gamewell said he had an edge on most of the moon-shiners for he had high-jumped six feet in high school and he could leap over about any fences he came across. Gamewell spent one year in the Federal Prison, but he was finally given a full pardon and his records were completely purged.

Then state Sen. Rembert Dennis made him an offer, 'stop running moonshine and I'll get you a job.'

"I told him, 'I quit'" Brown said. He became a constable for Magistrate Ira Grady, and later for Ira's son, Mel Grady. He also was commissioned as state constable in charge of litter prevention for South Carolina.

He retired from law enforcement many years ago, but he still kept the worn badge bearing his name in his wallet.

Chapter Thirty-Two

This is a true story that my dad told me as a boy and I recently checked it out with some of the man's kin-folks so here it is: Ira Palmer was a big, *mean*, man and most of the community were afraid of him. Some people said they would rather 'sandpaper a lions rear-end' than to tangle with this man. I remember him driving a wagon with a large umbrella attached to the seat, pulled by a little yellow colored mule. He lived in the Shulerville section of Berkeley County and had to drive past our house to get to the ole country store. He didn't like the hot sun shining on him during the summer so he kept an umbrella attached to his seat where he could ride in reasonable comfort.

We were told he had a boy who was very unruly. He tried his best but the boy just wouldn't do right, according to him. One day he took his boy hunting with him down by the swamp. The story goes that Ira shot and killed his boy and left him there for the animals to desecrate. This story was a hush-hush in the community and to my knowledge the law enforcement never knew about it.

This is a tribute to my grandad Harmon Shuler. He was born in 1852 and passed away in September 1940. He walked Planet Earth for eighty-eight years. I was sixteen years old at the time and I can still remember some of the tales he told to me.

Back then you didn't find out much about the civil war in history books, so I listened to my grand-dad. He said during the civil war brother fought against brother in a cause they thought was right. Thousands of men were killed in action and thousands more were wounded. When the war ended the men were fighting in Virginia. Some of them had horses but most of them had to walk home. They came back to a South ravaged by war. A lot of their towns, homes, and fields were burned. There wasn't much of a crop planted as all the able bodied men were fighting in the war.

There was no law as we know it today. Men in the community formed Vigilante Committees and when they heard about a man who wouldn't work or one who mistreated his family in any way they went to his house at night, pulled him outside and took him into the woods. They cut a good stick and put a whipping on the unfortunate man. He told me it was never necessary to go a second time as they gave him a good job on the first trip. Before this the people had regular whippings at the county seat. They would lock a man's hands and feet in holes in the wall, pull his shirt off and give him the necessary amount of lashes according to the crime he had committed. While Vigilantes was certainly not the answer to law and order, it served the purpose when there *was* no law and order.

A tribute to my mother: during World War II, the war department sent my mother a Gold Star to be displayed in the front window of our home. Any mother who had three or more boys in service during World War II, was classified as a Gold Star Mother. Of course, in my opinion, the government didn't have to make that distinction; I always knew my mom was a Gold Star Mother.

Mother's oldest son, Aaron F. Shuler was drafted in the service in 1942. He took basic training at McDill Air force Base near Tampa, Florida. He served with the engineers and spent most of his time on Okinawa in the South Pacific.

I was my Mother's next oldest son. I was drafted into the service in 1943. I took basic training in Fort McCellan, Alabama and trained with an anti-tank outfit. I served with Gen. Mark Clark's Fifth Army in Italy.

Mother's next oldest son, Jettie C. Shuler, enlisted in the Navy in 1944. He took his training in Florida and Maryland. He spent twenty-seven years in the navy and retired as Lieutenant Commander.

Mother's next oldest son, Timothy Monroe Shuler was drafted into the service in 1950. He served approximately two years in Korea, during the Korean War.

Mother's youngest son, James Everett Shuler was too young for World War II and the Korean War and too old for Viet Nam. He was a registered land surveyor and served as tax assessor in Berkeley County.

Chapter Thirty-Three

There is one section of Berkeley County referred to as 'Hell Hole'. There are no distinct lines or boundaries drawn on the area. To the best of my knowledge, while traveling eastward on 17 A, it begins somewhere on the West side of Jamestown and extends through Shulerville for many miles. You will also find 'Little Hell Hole' and 'Big Hell Hole' right in the same vicinity.

There is also an area known by the old timers as the Arm of Hell Hole. I have hunted deer in all the Hell Hole spaces and it is thick with Bay bushes and Bamboo vines. It is difficult for a man to make his way through it. Deer make small trails throughout the area and they lie down for cover. One day one of the men in our hunting party spotted a large buck going into the dense thicket of the Hell Hole. He must have only gone a short distance for he came out almost immediately. The man killed the deer and was surprised to find Bamboo vines hanging from the big buck's horns. The ole hunters referred to the areas as 'oceans'.

I have to say I think you will find some of the best people in the world in Hell Hole, South Carolina. They are proud of their heritage and will give you a big smile when you refer to them as 'Hellholians'.

Each year we celebrate by having a Hell Hole Festival in the town of Jamestown. It resembles a huge family reunion. It begins on a Friday and is a time for bar-b-que and chicken bog. Saturday is parade time. Everyone is welcome to attend and people come from all over. Each year a civic-minded individual over the age of 65 is selected to be governor of the event.

The festival's first formal ball was held in 1973. Cecil B. Guerry was founder of the Hell Hole Festival. E. F. 'Bullet' Guerry was the first governor. According to legend, the area was dubbed 'Hell Hole' after Revolutionary

War General Francis Marion made it through a clearing and told some of his men 'that is one hell of a hole.' Still others say it was named after a mysterious grassy clearing with a large hole in the middle of it where the general happened to fall into while scouting the area. After struggling to get out he was said to have called it the 'devil's workshop' thus it became 'Hell Hole'. I like both stories for they are a great reminder of the brave men who fought and won the freedom we enjoy today.

Hell Hole was put on the map during the depression years as 'The Moonshine Whiskey Capital of the Nation', rivaling the hometown of my friend Shirley Swiesz, from Harlan County Kentucky. We had buyers from all over the country coming to the Hell Hole area to get 'white lightening'. Jobs were scarce and there were few revenue agents; a perfect setting for making 'shine. Berkeley County's corn whiskey had a *good* taste. It was a clear liquid usually stored in a two quart jar, but a drink of 'shine would kick the unsuspecting like an ole mule. Bootleggers usually had testers and they could give you some high proof whiskey if you wanted it.

Practically all of the ole bootleggers have gone on to 'bootlegger heaven'. I suspect they are having a re-union there, telling their stories and listening to the ones that got caught and had to serve time. I hope they are separated from the revenuers though, for that would cause some by-gosh problems!

I was told by one of the ole timers that many of the revenue agents sent down to the Hell Hole Swamp area were never heard from again. The revenue agents got the upper hand on moon-shiners, though, when they started using piper cub airplanes to spot the stills from the air. A ground crew would be in a jeep with explosives while the airplanes searched for stills. When they found one they would fly in a circle over it until the ground crew arrived at the spot, with their dynamite. After several explosions anyone within hearing distance would know another moonshine still had bit the dust.

Joe Pruitt told me about the time he had a race with a Georgia revenuer. Ole Joe was making corn whiskey when the local law enforcement brought this fast running revenue agent from Georgia to try his luck at catching our local boot-leggers. It wasn't long before he had the goods on Joe and set out to catch him. The agent got behind ole Joe and within a few minutes the race was over. The agent caught Joe and threw him to the ground. But ole Joe wasn't going to give up without a fight. He kicked and lashed out at the agent until he finally pulled his revolver, cocked the hammer back and begged Joe in a calm voice, 'Please kick me just *one* more time.' Joe said "I could tell by the look on his face that he was gonna shoot me. I'm here to tell you, my mama didn't raise no fool!"

This land owner in Berkeley County told me that he hired a surveyor to make a survey of some land he had bought. The surveyor went to the courthouse and checked the records. When he had all the information he needed, he was ready to survey the property. He picked up the landowner and they headed for the woods.

They located the property, found all the corners and line trees which were properly marked but there turned out to be ten acres more than he had bought. This is normal when surveying old tracts of land as the older people stepped it off allowing three feet per step. They usually gave extra land in order to assure the buyer had the correct acreage. The deed always reads more or less to cover any mistakes. To get the exact acreage, you must have a surveyor to make a survey, thereby giving you the corner post position and to mark the line trees between corners. Then a plat is made of your property showing the exact footage from corner to corner and the location of the corners belonging to the adjoining land-owner.

Corner posts were usually made of lightwood knots or concrete with a cross and three bars under the cross. I was told by an old-timer that the cross represented Christ and the three bars represented the three days Christ lay in the tomb. Surveyors today usually use iron rods to make the corners.

This is a hunting story that happened to me when I was a boy. I was invited to go deer hunting with a group of men in an area near Santee River. We rode to the hunting area in an ole car, then took to our stands before the driver turned the dogs loose.

In just a few minutes the dogs jumped a deer and it headed toward me. They ran into a flock of wild turkeys, causing them to fly in fright. They came down in gunshot of me where I was standing on a pine ridge with no bushes for cover. I knew that turkeys have a sharp eye and the only chance I had was to stand very still. As I stood there watching them, two of these turkeys began to walk closer to me, stopping every few steps to stretch their necks and eyeball me.

I allowed the two turkeys to come as close as I dared before I started shooting them. Since we were deer hunting, I had my dad's Winchester automatic shotgun with three buckshot shells in it. I killed the first turkey with one shot, then turned on the other turkey with the remaining two shells. I crippled the turkey, breaking one wing and putting a buckshot through him. He started running and I ran behind him but could not catch him. He outran me flatfooted and the only way I caught him was because he got his broken wing hung up in some vines and could not get loose. I ran up to him and tried to catch him by the head as he struggled to get loose from the vines. Then he tried to peck me with his bill as this was his last way of defending himself. I finally got him by the head, pulled him loose from the vines, and rung his neck.

After taking care of the second turkey, I had trouble finding the first one as I had ran a good ways into the woods. Eventually I retrieved it and took them both back to my deer stand until the driver blew the horn, to signal to us that the hunt was over. The dogs and deer had headed toward the Santee River.

We got in the car and started home. The men planned to go back later for their dogs as they would run the deer to Santee River before they stopped and then it should take several hours before they got back to where we put them out.

When we got to my house I decided to be a good sport and offer one of my turkeys to the other hunters. The gentleman riding on the passenger side of the car held out his hand I gave him a turkey. He left there holding the turkey by the legs with a smile on his face. I really made his day.

Another time I was deer hunting and I saw my dogs run a doe deer into a patch of woods. As I was looking for her, I saw a six point buck with an eighteen inch spread, come out. I forgot all about the doe and killed him instead. I had his head mounted and I have had it in my den all these years.

On a hot day in the summer of 1943, I went deer hunting with my brothers and a friend on the Tiger Corner Road near Shulerville. The deer season was not in but we didn't care as the only seasons we knew were salt and pepper. To my knowledge there was only one game-warden patrolling this section of Berkeley County.

My brother took our dogs and was driving for deer on the left hand side of the road. My friend and I took two stands near the road. Before our dogs could strike a trail, we heard a pack of dogs running a deer, coming toward us from the Jamestown side of the Tiger Corner Road. I told my friend to take my stand and I would run further up the road if the dogs were leading past me. Sure enough, that is what happened. As I started running to cut the deer off, the deer had got well ahead of the dogs and he came out right where I had been standing. My friend started shooting down the road at the deer, missing it, but hitting me with two buck-shots.

One of these buck-shot hit me in the thigh and the other hit me in the heel, tearing up the heel of my shoe. My heel was hurting so badly, I didn't know at the time that I was hit in the thigh until the blood began running down my leg. I pulled off my pants and had my friend check my leg. The buckshot had made a hole in the fleshy part of my leg, but did not come out. There was a large blood shot circle around the hole in my thigh. We had to walk about three miles to get home. Fortunately, walking so far caused th bloodshot circle to disappear. I laid on my stomach while my brothers and friend got iodine, mercurochrome and turpentine, taking turns pouring them in my wounds. They kept down infection and after a couple of days, I bandaged them up with clean white cloth and they began the healing process. My grandmother was real sick at the time and my mother stayed with her for several days. I managed to keep the entire episode hid from my mother and didn't tell her for several years.

This story was told by my uncle. Back in the old days when cars weren't around, he went deer hunting with some friends on horseback. He said he rode his horse up to a pond in the woods and was sitting quietly, looking around, when he saw an ole mama alligator with a bunch of little alligators lying nearby on the bank of the pond. The natural instinct was to protect her young. She immediately started making peculiar noises, got up on her all fours, picked up her tail and started for my uncle. He put the spurs to his horse for a distance in order to get away from her. Normally a horse will spook under these conditions and throw the rider. After it was over, he said he thanked God his horse didn't throw him because he would probably have made a meal for the ole mama alligator and her youngsters had it done so.

Harold Peters was an old timer in the town of Bonneau, SC. He and his wife raised twelve children. When asked by someone why they had so many kids, his wife, Bertha, answered, "The train always came through Bonneau in the middle of the night. It woke him up and he would have a hard time going back to sleep. There ain't much to do at two or three o'clock in the morning when a body has insomnia."

Old Harold also told me about the time when he was driving near his home and saw a young lady sitting beside the road with her bicycle. He knew the woman so he stopped and asked her if he could be of any help to her. She replied, "If you have a two quart jar of whiskey and certain other qualifications, you can certainly help me!" He said, "No mam, I"m afraid I don't have either one." He left her where he found her.

Chapter Thirty-Four

Every book should have an ending so here is mine: Joe Trent was a nice, easy going fellow. He loved to hunt, fish and drink good moonshine whiskey. He made his own with an all copper outfit and he took a good deal of pride in it. He loved for his friends to come by his house, talk with him for a while and enjoy a good drink of 'shine.

One day he told me, "I have finally found the two most comfortable things in life, the first one is having a warm bathroom to use on a cold winter night...I hated out-houses when I was a boy... and the second one is being able to wear a loose pair of shoes." As the sun sets in Berkeley County, South Carolina, I feel sure those are important things to be thankful for and I am thankful for being here to write this book. I sincerely hope you have enjoyed reading it as much as I have enjoyed bringing these old tales and stories to the light of day. May the good Lord bless you that the rain will always fall gently upon your head and the wind will always be at your back...and may you always have the good nature to laugh at yourself from time to time.

Dennis Shuler

William Dennis Shuler with Shirley Noe Swiesz

About the Author

I was born in Shulerville on August 4th, 1924 and subsequently was raised on a small farm during the depression years. My father was killed when I was young while he was working on the Santee Cooper Dam, which was in the early stages of being built at that time. I was drafted into the Army on August 4th, 1943. I served twenty-eight months with the US Army. Eight months of that time was spent on the front lines. After being discharged, I joined my friends for a while, drawing twenty dollars per week unemployment and living the 'honky-tonk' life style. After several months, I enrolled in a barber college in Greenville, South Carolina. I followed this profession until May 1947 at which time I secured employment at Westvaco. I retired in 1987 and I am now operating a small farm in Berkeley County, which I bought in 1953. I guess when you think of it, I have been living the American Dream in my hometown in good ole Berkeley County, South Carolina!

Made in the USA
Columbia, SC
26 December 2023

29456477R00135